PENGUIN BOOKS
THE PROPHET OF PEACE

Courtesy Sanjay Austa

Maulana Wahiduddin Khan, president of the Islamic Centre, New Delhi, founded the Centre for Peace and Spirituality (CPS International) in 2001. These organizations are dedicated to presenting Islam in the modern idiom. The Maulana is the author of *The True Jihad*, *Islam Rediscovered*, *Islam and Peace* and numerous other best-selling books on Islam.

The Maulana received the Rajiv Gandhi Sadbhavna award in 2010.

The Prophet of Peace
Teachings of the
Prophet Muhammad

Maulana Wahiduddin Khan

PENGUIN BOOKS

PENGUIN BOOKS
Published by the Penguin Group
Penguin Books India Pvt. Ltd, 7th Floor, Infinity Tower C, DLF Cyber City,
Gurgaon 122 002, Haryana, India
Penguin Group (USA) Inc., 375 Hudson Street, New York, New York 10014, USA
Penguin Group (Canada), 90 Eglinton Avenue East, Suite 700, Toronto, Ontario,
M4P 2Y3, Canada
Penguin Books Ltd, 80 Strand, London WC2R 0RL, England
Penguin Ireland, 25 St Stephen's Green, Dublin 2, Ireland (a division of Penguin
Books Ltd)
Penguin Group (Australia), 707 Collins Street, Melbourne, Victoria 3008, Australia
Penguin Group (NZ), 67 Apollo Drive, Rosedale, Auckland 0632, New Zealand
Penguin Books (South Africa) (Pty) Ltd, Block D, Rosebank Office Park, 181 Jan
Smuts Avenue, Parktown North, Johannesburg 2193, South Africa

Penguin Books Ltd, Registered Offices: 80 Strand, London WC2R 0RL, England

First published in Penguin Books India 2009

Copyright © Maulana Wahiduddin Khan 2009

ISBN 9780143068174

Typeset in Dante MT by Eleven Arts, New Delhi
Printed at Thomson Press India Ltd, New Delhi

A PENGUIN RANDOM HOUSE COMPANY

Contents

Introduction

Terrorism is one of the gravest threats the world is facing today. The tragedy and irony of it is that most acts of armed violence by groups or individuals are being carried out in the name of religion, especially Islam.

Any terrorist, indeed any individual, can fulfil a given mission properly only when he is ideologically convinced of its validity. Ideology provides man with the necessary inspiration. Without an ideology, he fails to summon the requisite energy and enthusiasm so vital to the success of any struggle. This is as true of terrorism as it is of any other field of human endeavour.

Some countries are engaged in crushing terrorism in the name of Islam through military action, but that alone will not suffice to eliminate this phenomenon. Apart from often being armed to their teeth, today's terrorists are consumed by the ideology of their cause. So, engaging them is not simply an issue of gun versus gun. It has to be an issue of gun versus ideology.

Violence always begins in the mind; it needs to be uprooted therefore from the mind itself. We have to find an ideology of peace with which to confront the ideology of violence; without that there will be no end to the violence. The horrendous events that took place in New York and Washington on 11 September 2001 are adequate proof of this point. They effectively demonstrated that, with a violent bent of mind, man can wage a war without even being in possession of arms. He can bombard without a bomb. Therefore, we have to eradicate the violent mindset and inculcate instead a peaceful way of thinking.

Let us not forget that where even a superpower cannot afford an endless war, the terrorist can. Terrorists are people of a different breed; their ultimate goal is not necessarily victory. Death too is a desired goal. According to their self-devised ideology, they believe that if they die in a militant struggle, they will instantly enter Paradise. Thus, for them, both victory and defeat have equal value—in either case, they believe that they are the winners. On the strength of this misleading ideology, terrorists can sustain their militancy for an indefinite period of time, even for many generations. But although they belong to a different breed, they are not a people apart. They are an integral part of the contemporary society they live in. And the greatest source of their strength is the ideological factory they run, aimed at brainwashing the youth. This brainwashing process goes on unceasingly, and there is always a long queue of those who want to be recruited and end up as martyrs.

Terrorism will persist in one form or another until the ideology of violence is countered with another ideology based on peace. But let us first understand the ideology of violence that is resulting in terrorism. This ideology is that Islam is a political system and that it is the duty of all Muslims to establish the political rule of Islam in the world. This kind of thinking was not prevalent during the time of Prophet Muhammad or his early companions. It is a later innovation. This was developed over the last few centuries by a handful of people and has become widespread in the Muslim world today. This has led to the present-day violence.

A large number of Muslims, especially many among the youth, have become obsessed with this ideology and are trying to establish the political rule of Islam, thinking it to be their ticket to Paradise. Having failed to achieve this objective of establishing Islamic rule by peaceful methods, they have started resorting to suicide bombing. The reasoning behind this seems to be 'If we cannot eliminate non-Islamic rule, let us at least destabilize it and pave the way for Islamic rule'.

After studying Islam by referring to its original sources— the Quran and the teachings of Prophet Muhammad (the Hadith)—one can say with certainty that the political interpretation of Islam is an innovation and the real Islam, as followed by Prophet Muhammad and his early followers, is based upon peace, compassion and tolerance.

A new strategy must now be adopted, a strategy that requires developing a full-fledged ideology of peace to counter the ideology of violence. The ideology of violence is prevalent all over the world and is so deep-rooted in the minds of not only the extremists but also of many common Muslims that it is important to expose this ideology for what it is and show in detail how it contradicts Quranic teachings. Everyone will thus see the stark difference between the two.

Time and again, throughout the ages, people have risen in rebellion and made their mark on human history, but seldom did they attain the level that the 'Islamists' of today have taken it to. There are two main reasons for this state of events—modern weaponry and modern media. These are the twin factors that have propelled terrorism into the limelight.

In earlier times there were neither aeroplanes nor 110-storey buildings. That is why no person could conspire to hijack aeroplanes and crash them into high-rise buildings. This has become feasible only with modern technological progress and development. Moreover, it is only very recently that it has become possible for such events to be televised *as they take place* and to be communicated by the media almost instantly to people all over the world. The plain truth is that a terrorist is an ordinary human being; and if he has been accorded the status of an internationally acclaimed militant activist, it is thanks in no small measure to modern technology.

Another aspect of this phenomenon which must be questioned is the terrorist's ideology. The extremists call their terrorist culture 'Islamic jihad'—clearly a misnomer—and portray their actions as having been carried out under the banner of Islam. In this manner, the religion of Islam gets falsely linked with terrorist activities, and its name gets besmirched. It was repeated acts of terrorism that led the *Daily Times*, London, to study Islam with reference to bin Laden, and then, upholding sensationalism over objectivity, produce an article entitled 'A Religion That Sanctions Violence'.

Contrary to common belief, Islam, by definition, is a religion of peace. The very word 'Islam' (from the Arabic *silm*) means 'peace'. According to a tradition of the Prophet, 'Peace is Islam',[1] in other words, peace is a prerequisite of Islam. The same is stated in the Hadith:

> 'A Muslim is one from whose tongue and hands people are safe.'[2]

Further, one of the attributes of God mentioned in the Quran (59:23) is *As-Salam*, which means 'peace and security'. Thus, God's Being itself is a manifestation of peace. Indeed, 'God is Peace'.[3] The Quran (5:16) likens divine guidance to the paths of peace. Paradise, which is the ideal human abode, is called the 'Home of Peace' (10:25). It is also said that the people of Paradise will wish one another peace— this indicates that the social culture of the people of Paradise will be based on peace.

At a three-day symposium held at the American University in Washington, in February 1998, I made a speech on 'Islam and Peace', where I said:

> It is no exaggeration to say that Islam and violence are contradictory to each other. The concept of Islamic violence is so obviously unfounded that prima facie it stands rejected. The fact that violence

is not sustainable in the present world is sufficient indication that violence as a principle is quite alien to the scheme of things in Islam. Islam claims to be an eternal religion and, as such, could never afford to uphold any principle which could not stand up to the test of time. Any attempt to bracket violence with Islam amounts therefore to casting doubt upon the very eternity of the Islamic religion. 'Islamic terrorism' is a contradiction in terms, much like 'pacifist terrorism'. The truth of the matter is that all the teachings of Islam are based directly or indirectly on the principle of peace.

As regards suicide bombings, according to Islam, life is so precious that it should never be terminated at one's will on any pretext. Islam is a harbinger of life. It has no room for death. That is why the principle of patience is given the utmost importance in Islam.

The problem is that while the study of Islam always used to be done with reference to the Quran, it is now being done with reference to terrorist activities and the ideology that supports them. This calls for an objective review so that a proper distinction may be made between Islam and the politically motivated 'Islamic terrorism'.

This book takes an objective view of the self-styled jihadi terrorist movements and attempts to examine how these movements stand in relation to the Islamic ideology based on the Quran and the Hadith—the original sources of Islam.

This book may be regarded as a study of Islam with reference to terrorism, or, conversely, as a study of terrorism with reference to Islam. Today, both issues are so closely interlinked as to be almost inseparable. The study of one becomes the study of the other.

The terrorists have concocted a wrong interpretation of the Quran; this interpretation has it that the killing of non-Muslims whom they refer to as *kafirs* is an act of worship and a guarantee of entry into Paradise. The movement of the terrorists is a movement against humanity. To put an end to this movement, what is required is to bring about a de-conditioning of its adherents. This can be done only by meeting them on an intellectual level and impressing upon them the true and positive picture of Islam based on the ideology of peace rather than on their deceitful ideology of violence.

1
A Blinkered Approach
to History

There are two methods of studying history. One is to look at history in the light of universally discernible trends, and the other to see it purely in the context of the evolution of some nation or race. The phenomenon of terrorism is born when history is not seen in the light of broad historical developments, but exclusively in relation to one's own nation or community. In that case, we are dealing with only a single area of relevance and do not consider all the pertinent facts. Perhaps the most serious instance of this approach to the study of history has been the approach taken by many modern Muslim leaders, as a result of which religious terrorism has come into existence.

In the twelfth century the greater part of the known inhabited world was ruled by Muslims. With the spread of Western colonialism, which came in the wake of the Renaissance, Muslim dominion began to crumble; the Western powers managed to establish their ascendancy either directly or indirectly in all Muslim countries. In the spheres of culture, economics, politics, indeed, in every sphere, Muslims found themselves in a state of subservience. This feeling of victimhood has persisted in the collective Muslim mind right up to the twenty-first century, despite there being nearly fifty Muslim-majority nations in the world today.

In hindsight, the change of power, which was a result of changed historical circumstances, was ineluctable. But present-day Muslim leaders were not prepared to accept the changed state of affairs. Consequently, they developed a mentality of resistance, which gave birth to terrorism with all its horrifying manifestations.

It is a matter of historical record that in 597 BC, Nebuchadnezzar II, a Babylonian ruler, attacked Jerusalem, took the Jews living there prisoners, put an end to Jewish rule and took possession of Palestine. After this tragedy, the Jewish prophet Jeremiah simply said to the Jews:

> 'Say to the king and to the queen mother, "Humble yourselves; sit down. For your rule shall collapse, even the crown of your glory."' (Jeremiah 13:18)

It was God Himself who had put an end to Jewish rule in Palestine and brought about the establishment of the rule of the king of Babylon. But the Jews, seeing no historical inevitability in this change of power, attributed it to the tyranny of the Babylonian king. That was why, unable to accept the passing of the reins of their country into foreign hands, they engaged in destructive actions against their new king. This only resulted in the further decimation of the Jews.

These actions have been repeated by Muslims in modern times. It is strange that they have learned no lessons from

Jewish history, and have repeatedly made the same mistakes as the Jews, only with much greater fervour. Needless to say, their actions have yielded similarly dismal results.

The domination of Muslim states by foreign powers was a historical event similar to that which the Bible describes as taking off the crown of glory. In this case, what Muslims should have done was to accept this change as the will of God. But, swayed by their emotional leaders, they came to see this new situation not as the handiwork of a divine act, but as part of a conspiracy of dominant nations; they regarded it as a usurpation and a tyranny. As a result, Muslims, for the greater part, started developing an attitude of hatred towards the Western nations. Almost all Muslim writers and speakers began giving vent to their sentiments in the language of grievance and protest.

When Muslim intelligentsia descended into negativism of this kind, it was but natural that Muslims in general lapsed into a violent way of thinking. Inevitably, this gave rise to a culture of violence that culminated in extremist activities in which the use of firearms became common, as also means such as hijacking and suicide bombing. It was this state of affairs in Muslim society that led directly to the perpetrators of violence against the West acquiring the status of heroes in the Muslim world.

2

History from a Muslim Perspective

History, with its combination of events and their underlying causes, can be viewed from different angles. To understand the phenomenon of 'Islamic terrorism', we shall have to look at history from a Muslim perspective.

This does not mean placing it within the context and framework of any form of dogmatism. An in-depth study of any subject requires an examination of the historical aspects relevant to it, and so it is but natural that the researcher will adopt a selective method, that is, he or she will eliminate certain elements of history as being irrelevant to the aim of the study in question and will include other parts as being relevant thereto. With this universal principle of study in mind, the attempt here is to present an Islamic overview of the four relevant stages of history: the stage of worship of the phenomena of nature; the stage of worship of God; the stage of conquest of nature; and the stage of Muslim anger.

Islam emerged at the turn of the seventh century AD. History shows that for thousands of years prior to that man had worshipped nature. The sun, the moon, the earth and all other phenomena of nature are God's creations, just as man is. These phenomena were created as a support system for man. And they exist so that man might harness them for his service. But man, holding them to be divine beings and creators instead of mere creations, began worshipping them. As a result of this reverence for nature, all kinds of superstitions took root and pervaded all aspects of human life. Kings, who were mere humans, were accorded divine status.

The truth is that this all-pervasiveness of superstition served as a hurdle to all kinds of human development. Placing nature upon a pedestal of sanctity had completely discouraged an investigation of it. Without such investigation, scientific and industrial progress was simply not possible. This is why the concept of polytheism becomes an obstacle to human advancement.

The concept of polytheism gave birth to many odd beliefs and spawned a whole series of superstitions. For instance, lightning was taken to be a god's fiery wand. The eclipse of the sun or moon was taken to be the work of some malign force, or attributed to some deity who had been beset by the powers of darkness, and so on.

The polytheistic concept of sanctity proved highly advantageous to religious leaders, who developed the accompanying superstitions into a whole set of 'religious' beliefs. Through these, they began to exploit people by making them believe that they (the religious leaders) were intermediaries between God and man. They encouraged the idea that to please them was, indirectly, to please God. The greatest benefit of all was reaped by the kings. Exploiting this mentality, which had been conditioned in the people, they developed the concept of the god-king. In any society, the king is the richest and most powerful. He is distinguished in many other respects too from the common people. Taking advantage of this distinctive status, the kings instilled into the minds of the people that they were superior to common man, that they were, in fact, God's representatives on earth. Some said that they were a link between God and man. Others went further and pretended to be incarnations of God on earth. As such, they were supposed to possess supernatural powers. They managed, in consequence, to wield absolute power over their subjects.

In the seventh century AD Islam came upon the scene. The monotheism it preached brought about a revolution, ending the age of superstition. As a result, the practice of worshipping natural phenomena and according divine status to kings was discontinued. Acknowledging this revolutionary event, the Belgian historian Henri Pirenne observed: 'Islam changed the face of the globe. The traditional order of history was overthrown.'

But this was only a stage in history and not an end in itself. Muslims did bring to an end the age of nature worship, but they could not take man to the next stage of history. This stage was to discover the powers latent within nature and harness them for man's service.

This latter task was performed by the West. It was the Western nations that discovered the hidden powers of nature and put them to human service, thus taking history to the next stage.

For instance, steam power was latent in water, but Muslims did not discover this property of water. Machines could be built from the minerals in the earth, but Muslims, never having had an industrial revolution in their midst, had no inkling of mineral-laden earth and thus were unable to take humanity into the modern age. Petrol had the potential of energy, but Muslims failed to discover a way to process and utilize it for the progress of human civilization. All the unique elements of communications technology were inherent in nature, but discovering them and stepping into the age of modern communications were done by the West alone.

In the nineteenth and the twentieth centuries when Western nations displaced Muslim hegemony, it was, in fact, historical forces that displaced Muslims from the pedestal of power and given this seat to Western nations. This was so because the Western nations demonstrated that they were more deserving, and that they could take man to the next stage of history. Latter-day events have proved that this verdict of history was right: Western nations were, indeed, competent to further human progress.

Such changes in reign were not effected smoothly. They were inevitably marked by social upheavals, because of which people failed to appreciate their real nature. Becoming victims of misunderstanding, they went through the trauma of unwarranted and uncalled-for reactions.

Indeed, when such political reshuffling takes place, the subjugated would not go down without a fight. That is why Muslim empires, right from their first flush of victory till their last defeat, continuously faced revolts from those they subjugated; although these were not as effective as modern-day rebellions. The rebels of yore did not have the military resources of their contemporary counterparts.

When Muslim writ ran over the world, those that it subjugated launched what they called 'liberation' movements against their Muslim rulers. Muslim historians regarded this as rebellion. Today, when Muslims find themselves subjugated by Western nations, they have launched what they term jihad against those they see as their oppressors. The West views this as terrorism. On the face of it, nothing seems to have changed—only the terminology is different. There is, however, a significant difference between the military capabilities of yesterday's crusaders and today's jihadis—technological progress has ensured that modern-day terrorists pack a far deadlier punch than the rebels of yore.

We have called the fourth stage the period of Muslim anger. Although there are around fifty independent Muslim states today, they have not been able to further their progress due to the negative mindset of the majority. That is why, in spite of having political freedom, they continue to be dominated by Western nations. Thus, their anger against Western nations has yet to subside. In one form or the other, it continues to surface from time to time.

This negative expression of anger has proved to be an obstacle to the progress and development of Muslims. Whatever the extremists have done, or are doing in the form of violent activity, has only resulted in creating a nuisance factor for Western nations. In effect, the anger evinced by present-day Muslims is only contributing to their own destruction.

Islam teaches result-oriented action. Fruitless action has no place in its philosophy. As the consequences of terrorist action are synonymous with self-destruction, Muslims are duty-bound to desist from it. It is, therefore, vital that the jihadis of today put a complete and immediate stop to their ineffective jihadi activities and, by a process of introspection, make a total reassessment of their course of action, so that they may seriously replan their own future.

3

Rediscovering Islam

There are two bases from which movements in the name of Islam can be launched. One is through the study of the Quran and the Hadith, combined with the endeavour to understand Islam from the life of Prophet Muhammad, resulting in the discovery of Islam as an absolute truth. The other is through the rediscovery of national pride in Islam and then the projection of this concept to the world at large.

In the first case, one is inevitably moved to convey this discovery of Islam to others and to convince them of its truth. One who adopts this method cannot but revive the original spirit of Islam. A movement of this positive nature is, in essence, truly Islamic.

But, starting out from the second basis—even if one is imbued with the values of Islam from birth—what one actually accomplishes is the fostering of overweening pride and the building up of a narrow sense of partisanship. It is this latter notion of Islam which was implicitly held up as an ideal by General Zia-ul Haq, former president of Pakistan, in the speech he made at the United Nations General Assembly in New York on 1 October 1980: 'As they enter the 15th century of Islamic History, the Islamic peoples have rediscovered their pride in their religion, their great culture and their unique social and economic institutions.'

This concept of Islam is, in reality, parochial in nature and derives not from the Quran and the Hadith, but rather from the resounding victories of the Muslim past. Seen in the context of the splendours of Muslim history, Islam has become a matter of pride for Muslims. Today most Muslims live with a sense of the glory of the shared Islamic community or *ummah*. This sense of pride in Islam, a phenomenon of supra-national history, is something that inspires, energizes and activates most Muslims today. Therefore, when any group resorts to actions aimed at demolishing Muslim pride, Muslims immediately feel provoked and launch a movement directed against that group—in the name of Islam.

In modern times, all such movements have, in fact, been instigated as a matter of reaction, arising in the wake of some attack on the communal pride of Muslims, rather than out of any real sense of the discovery of God. The phenomenon of 'Islamic terrorism', which has little to do with the discovery of God, is one such glaring example. God-fearing Muslims, unlike the terrorists, follow in the footsteps of their Prophet of whom the Quran says:

'Did He not find you wandering, and give you guidance?' (93:7)

That is, God found Muhammad intent on finding the truth, but in a quandary as to which way to turn, so He showed him the right path. This quest for truth, coupled with the willingness to be guided by the Almighty, is the model to be followed. If anyone is to be judged on the purity of his Islam, he has to first measure up to this Muhammadan model.

Prophet Muhammad ibn Abdullah was not a non-Muslim by birth. He belonged to the religion of Abraham, just as today's Muslims belong to the religion of Muhammad. But as we learn from the Quran, that Muhammad ibn Abdullah ibn Abdul Muttalib had been born into the religion of Abraham was not any great source of satisfaction to him, as the religion had by then been distorted from a monotheistic religion into a polytheistic one. It was this violation of a cherished ideal that caused the Prophet to become a genuine seeker after truth. A considerable part of his life was then directed towards this goal, until he reached the age of forty. It was at that point that God began to guide him. Thus, Muhammad rediscovered the original divine religion.

What every Muslim and every Muslim leader ought to do, first and foremost, is to rediscover Islam. Without this rediscovery, no Muslim is deserving of divine guidance and ultimate salvation, nor does he or she have the right to launch any movement in the name of Islam or become a leader of Muslims.

The lives of the terrorists, their colleagues and supporters show that their experiences and aspirations do not measure up to the Muhammadan standard. They have never undergone the long wandering in search of truth, and they have launched their 'Islamic' movement without any rediscovery of Islam. Seen from this perspective, the objectives and actions of the terrorists and their supporters deserve to be rejected outright. Never having made any serious attempt to discover Islam, they have no right to lay claim to leadership in the name of Islam.

For all human beings, the realization of Islam is the discovery of God, rather than the mere fact of being of Muslim lineage. When an individual discovers Islam as an absolute truth, he makes that his starting point. Being born into a Muslim family and thus having a Muslim name certainly makes one a member of a social organization of Muslims, but in no way does it entitle anyone to find his or her name on the list of the 'guided ones' in the true Quranic sense.

The basic weakness of those such as the terrorists waging their war in the name of Islam is their failure to discover Islam as an eternal truth. Their Islam has been derived from Muslim political history, rather than from the realization of God. This being so, they themselves are merely bit players in Muslim history. That is why they fail to render any genuine service to Islam, in spite of the enormous struggle on their part.

Experience shows that the version of Islam that bases itself on the pride of belonging to a certain group or community produces a negative mentality. This has led to a situation where the Muslim communities bear grudges against or are in rivalry with one another. In this world, every community has experienced oppression or injustice inflicted on it by some other community at one time or another. On account of this, it almost always happens that negativism remains uppermost in the minds of the oppressed community or group and it becomes a permanent mindset.

A discovery of the true Islam leads, on the other hand, to an entirely different attitude. One who has discovered Islam in the true sense becomes a positive thinker in the highest sense of the word. Complaints and grievances become irrelevant to him. For such a person, 'we' and 'they' become one. Cases of oppression and atrocities are then regarded as a result of the law of nature. One who has attained a realization of Islam regards these as a part of God's creation plan, rather than as resulting from the nefarious designs of some supposed enemy.

Regrettably, the majority of present-day Muslim leaders think along these lines. Each one of them is bent upon airing his grievances against so-called enemies and all their efforts are directed towards revealing the supposed plots of enemy nations. In the process, they fill the hearts and minds of Muslims with hatred. Jihad is but a particularly virulent expression of this hatred. Hatred is nothing but passive violence.

If, on the contrary, these leaders had rediscovered the absolute truth of Islam sent for all humanity, they would be filled with feelings of benevolence towards humanity. They would see such experiences that they now consider negative in a positive light. An approach of this sort would produce universality of thought, and, as a result, Muslims would strive for the preservation and prosperity of humanity rather than for its destruction.

4

The Quran's Plan for Man

The aim of the Quran—with its 6000-plus verses spread over 114 chapters—is to develop a man who would possess the two sublime qualities of being a worshipper of God and a well-wisher of mankind. According to Quranic philosophy, human life is intertwined with God and mankind. On the one hand is God, his Creator, and on the other are human beings among whom he has to lead his life from the moment of his birth until his death. The Quran encourages man to have sublime feelings for God and to reflect these sentiments in the way he worships Him. At the same time, it is made clear to him that in his heart he must also have feelings of benevolence and compassion for humanity at large. To be a true Muslim requires a combination of these two virtues.

The Quran tells us that God has given innumerable blessings to humanity. Man, as he benefits from this divine bounty, is duty-bound to proffer thanks to his Benefactor. He is bidden to love and fear God more than anyone or anything else, and ought to consider himself accountable to God.

Another of man's responsibilities, according to the Quran, is to be unfailingly just in his treatment of other human beings. His life among his fellow men must be one of total honesty. He must fulfil others' needs, living among people in such a way that his actions are of benefit to all. He must be a giver and not a taker. His character should reflect modesty, not arrogance. He should not allow himself to react to provocation, but should rather tread the path of patience and avoidance of conflict. He must be conscious that others have a share in his time and in his earnings. In short, the Quran's desire for man is to make him a complex-free soul or a soul at peace (89:27).

The Quran emphasizes the formation of one's character through introspection and moulding oneself to the will of God. Nowhere does it enjoin the believer to engage in violence, leading to the destruction of fellow human beings.

The Quran tells us, moreover, that the present world is intended to be a testing ground, specially designed for the trial of mankind, for God wants to see whether people are capable of leading their lives in accordance with His will. It is their conduct on earth that will determine whether or not they are deserving of Paradise in the next, eternal stage of life after death.

According to the Quran, Paradise is another name for God's neighbourhood, and in this neighbourhood only those who are sincere in their belief in God and have compassion and love for God's servants will find acceptance.

God has the same compassionate relationship with every man as a father has with all his children. Therefore, it is alien to the divine scheme of creation that this earthly plane should be marred by hatred, killing and violence. It is God's most cherished desire that love should be returned for hatred, and violence should be met with peace.

The terrorists want to destroy or disrupt the divine scheme by creating disorder and fear in a world intended by God to be free of such things. They attempt to prevent people from receiving a share in God's mercy by placing obstacles in their path. All such actions—carried out in the name of God—are actually against the will of God, and will never bring them any divine reward. Undeserving as they are, on the Day of Judgement, they will be taken to the enclosures of the sinners where God will call them to account for indulging in acts of violence against His servants in contradiction to His will as expressed in the Quran.

5

The Islamic Model

The Quran says:

> 'You have indeed in the Prophet of God a good example.' (33:21)

This means that Islam has given Muhammad ibn Abdullah to the world as a shining example and has established him as a role model for all time to come. All those who claim to be Muslims are therefore honour-bound to follow in his footsteps.

Some Muslims attempt to legitimize the movements launched by them by calling them 'Muhammadi' or 'Islamic'. But if in doing so they deviate, even by the slightest, from the Prophetic norm, they are certain to be rejected as unworthy by God.

All Muslim terrorists fall into this category of the unworthy. They call themselves Muslims and justify their actions by misinterpreting the Quran and the Hadith, thus setting themselves up as role models for other Muslims. But surely, they are aware that it is to Prophet Muhammad, and to no one else, that this status has been given by Islam. Far from serving as role models for others, they, like all believers, will also be judged on their conformance to the Prophetic model. It is this model that will determine who follows the path of Islam and who has deviated from it.

To understand how Islamists have deviated from the right path by becoming violent extremists, we must look into the life of the Prophet, which reveals that in personal matters he was an idealist, but in social matters he staunchly upheld the status quo. However, the 'positive status quoism' of Prophet Muhammad should not be equated with passivity; it should be understood rather as a deliberate plan of action. What it actually meant was the avoidance of conflict so as to leave him free to exploit available opportunities to spread the word of God in a peaceful and non-confrontational manner.

There is one particular example of the Prophet's method of 'positive status quoism' that stands out. Prophet Muhammad began his missionary work in Makkah in AD 610. At that time the sacred sanctuary of Makkah, the Kabah, which was supposed to be solely for the worship of the one true God, housed no less than 360 idols. The continuing presence of these idols could very well have jeopardized his entire mission to spread the message that God was one, that He alone was worthy of worship and that idolatry was forbidden by Him.

Muslims believe that this sanctuary had been built by Prophet Abraham for the purpose of worshipping the one true God, 4000 years ago. But over the centuries, the

Makkans had lost sight of Abraham's objective and had placed in it 360 idols worshipped by different tribes. (This, in fact, suited the purpose of the Makkans, because it allowed them to establish their leadership over all these different groups.) It would appear then that the first issue to be settled by the Prophet would have been the removal of all the idols from the Kabah.

But that was not his way; he decided instead to treat this state of affairs as an opportunity to further his own mission. He saw this regular assembly of Makkans and people from different tribes in the courtyard of the Kabah to worship the idols as a great opportunity to preach the teachings of the Quran. And so, by refusing to take issue with the presence of the idols, he was able to convey the truth of monotheism to large numbers of people. This is what I meant by 'positive status quoism'.

A very similar situation prevailed in the town of Bamiyan in Afghanistan in 2001. Two colossal statues of Gautam Buddha had been carved into the side of a cliff there in the sixth century AD. These were historical masterpieces, which attracted a steady stream of tourists. Buddhists in particular came there in large numbers from all over the world.

If the Taliban, who had taken control of that area, had only stopped to consider it, they could have seized upon this situation as a great opportunity to propagate the teachings of Islam to the world at large. They could have come into contact with innumerable people in a very natural way and peacefully gone on with their missionary work.

But the political mindset of the Taliban had rendered them incapable of deeper understanding of the matter. Muslim extremists usually think that their first task is to remove all visible manifestations of un-Islamic culture and any supposed obstacles to the prevalence of Islam, even if they have to resort to violence to do so. The Taliban could not therefore go beyond thinking that the Buddha statues were idols and thus it was their religious duty to purify their land by demolishing them. So they blew them up with dynamite. Far from receiving any benefit from this move, they only managed to antagonize the entire modern world. This action totally belied the Prophet's example. Had the Taliban truly followed in his footsteps, they would have left the statues intact and would have emulated the strategy the Prophet had adopted in Makkah.

Another example from the life of Prophet Muhammad that present-day Muslim leaders might do well to follow is the attitude he adopted towards the tribal parliament called Dar-an-Nadwa in Makkah, of which Abdul Muttalib, his grandfather, was a member. Considering the political power enjoyed by this institution in Arabia, it might have been expected that Prophet Muhammad, as an emerging religious and social leader, would follow historical precedent and attempt to take control of it, or at least demand that the vacant seat of Abdul Muttalib be given to him. But throughout his thirteen years in Makkah, Prophet Muhammad did no such thing. Displaying total disinterest in this political institution, he concentrated on working peacefully for the success of his mission.

Unlike the Prophet, many present-day Muslim leaders and reformers consider that they must capture political power or at least gain access to it, come what may. Regardless of which country they are in, they have directed all their efforts towards bringing political centres under their influence, and will not stop at anything to bring about the total destruction of those that oppose them in their endeavours.

But this kind of political initiative is completely at variance with the example set by Prophet Muhammad. That is why it must be totally rejected. Unfortunately we can find instances of such deviant behaviour in every Muslim country—Saudi Arabia, Egypt, Syria, Sudan, Afghanistan, Pakistan, Iran, indeed, all over the globe.

Another instance of the Prophet's exemplary conduct was in the way he tackled the stiff opposition he had to face from Makkan polytheists—who were plotting to kill him. At that time Prophet Muhammad could either have gathered his companions and fought a pitched battle against the Makkans or gone underground and secretly engaged in destructive activities against them. But he opted for neither of these courses. Instead, he left Makkah and went to Madinah, which was about 300 miles away. And there he again devoted himself to spreading the word of Islam.

Given the circumstances of Prophet Muhammad's departure from Makkah, it might have been expected that the Prophet would have told the Madinans stories of Makkan oppression in order to gain their support. On the contrary, Prophet Muhammad did not utter a single word against the Makkans. Instead, he sedulously reminded

Madinans of the reality of the life Hereafter. On reaching Madinah, he confined himself to saying:

'O people! Save yourself from the chastisement of the Hereafter, even if it be by a piece of date.'[1]

Prophet Muhammad was more concerned about saving people from God's punishment than about gaining sympathy for himself over the persecution he had suffered at the hands of his own townspeople.

Evidently, 'Islamic terrorists' are far removed from the path of the Prophet, for, through the media, they are disseminating vicious propaganda against supposed enemies all over the world. This attitude deserves total rejection, for it flies in the face of the example provided by Prophet Muhammad.

Such extremists would do well to consider how the Prophet behaved when in AD 622 he reached Madinah, and found that of the tribes inhabiting the town a certain number were Jewish. The Prophet, far from harming the Jews in any way, attempted to establish good relations between them and the Muslims. Towards this end, during his initial days in Madinah, the Prophet went to the extent of making the Jewish *qibla* (direction for prayer) the qibla for Muslims too. Later, Makkah became the qibla.

In this connection, there is another instance of his broad-mindedness that is worth mentioning. One day in Madinah, the Prophet saw a funeral procession passing by. He immediately stood up as a mark of deference. One of his companions remarked:

"'O Prophet of God, this was the funeral of a Jew, not a Muslim." To this the Prophet responded: "Was he not a human being?"'[2]

This incident tells us that the Prophet regarded all human beings as equal. Regardless of religious or political differences, he had equal respect in his heart for all. The Prophet recognized each individual's right to personal dignity.

True to his character, when Prophet Muhammad left Makkah for Madinah, he did not start preparations for war against his Makkan opponents or launch a propaganda campaign against them. Instead, he immediately engaged in constructive activities in his new place of residence, for instance, the construction of a place of worship; establishing links of brotherhood between Makkan emigrants and Madinan Muslims; creating an environment of tolerance and mutual respect between followers of different religions; spreading the moral teachings of the Quran; and striving to build a righteous society in Madinah.

An equally important task undertaken by him was to bring to cessation the violent confrontations between tribes which were a part of life in ancient Arabia. The religion of Prophet Muhammad was monotheistic, whereas at that time, the whole of Arabia practised polytheism. For this reason, the Prophet should, by the conventions of his time, have been at war with all of Arabia. But, through strategic planning, he pacified the entire peninsula. He did this by sending out delegations from Madinah to the various tribes living in different parts of the country for the purpose of negotiating peace treaties with them.

The occasions on which the Prophet actually faced armed confrontation were very few and far between. And these took place because of offensive action on the part of the Quraysh tribe. The Prophet was compelled to engage in some skirmishes with them for the first time in the field of Badr in the second year of his emigration. After this battle, their armies met again at Uhud in 3 AH, at Khaybar in 7 AH and at Hunayn in 8 AH. Save these four very short battles, he did not enter into any major conflict with the Quraysh or their allies. It should be emphasized that each of the four battles—Badr, Uhud, Khaybar and Hunayn—lasted for only half a day. Indeed, the Islamic revolution through which Islam made a peaceful entry into Arabia in the eighth year of Hijrah,[3] starting with the city of Makkah, incurred so little loss of life that it may be rightly regarded as a peaceful rather than a violent revolution.

Unfortunately, we find today's 'Islamic terrorists' acting in a manner entirely contrary to the example set by the Prophet. Where the Prophet adopted the policy of avoidance of war by planning for peace, the terrorists plan to destroy the peace of the world by their violent militant actions. How great a moral abyss lies between the Prophet and those who claim to be his followers!

It is worth noting that the secret of the Prophet's extraordinary success in promulgating monotheism lay not only in the ideological power of his mission, but also in the entirely peaceful methods which he adopted.

6

A Prophet of Peace

Historians have generally acknowledged that the Prophet of Islam, Muhammad ibn Abdullah ibn Abdul Muttalib, was extremely successful during his lifetime. For instance, the British historian Edward Gibbon (1735–94) pays tribute to Prophet Muhammad in his book *The History of the Decline and Fall of the Roman Empire* when he observes that 'the rise and expansion of Islam was one of the most memorable revolutions, which has impressed a new and lasting character on the nations of the globe'.

M.N. Roy (1887–1954), an Indian leader, writes in his book *The Historical Role of Islam* (1939) that Muhammad must be recognized as by far the greatest of all the prophets and that the expansion of Islam was 'the most miraculous of all miracles'.

Dr Michael Hart, in his book titled *The 100* (1978), has made a list—choosing from the entire span of human history—of 100 individuals whose achievements are the most outstanding. At the head of this list of high achievers, he puts the name of Prophet Muhammad. He writes: 'He is the only man in history, who was supremely successful on both the religious and secular levels.'

So, what was the secret of this great success achieved by the Prophet? The secret lies in one word—peace. It would not be overstating the case to say that Prophet Muhammad was the greatest peace activist in history. He exploited peace as an unconquerable force, for, as the Quran says:

'Reconciliation is the best.' (4:128)

Prophet Muhammad once said:

'God grants to peace, what he does not grant to violence.'[1]

Leo Tolstoy once wrote: 'All the revolutions in history are only examples of the more wicked seizing power and oppressing the good.'[2]

If this is indeed the case, then the revolution brought about by Prophet Muhammad may be considered a remarkable exception, for the Islamic revolution brought about the exact opposite of Tolstoy's pronouncement. Students of history might arrive at conclusions that differ from mine. However, I feel that those would mostly be the result of inadequate study, and that when research is undertaken on a vaster and more comprehensive scale, any diversity of opinion automatically narrows down. On the basis of my research, I am of the opinion that in view of the contribution made to human history by Prophet Muhammad, he can be most appropriately called the Prophet of Peace. Indeed, in the Quran (21:107), Prophet Muhammad is called the Prophet of Mercy, which is only another name for the Prophet of Peace—both express the same reality in different words.

Here is an example to illustrate this point. Some defensive battles took place during the lifetime of the Prophet, one of which was fought at Badr. The traditions tell us that when the battle was taking place, Prophet Muhammad was sitting some distance away from the battlefield in a makeshift camp. He was seen drawing some lines on the sand. Major Akbar Khan, a writer, making the assumption that his actions must relate to the battle, observed, 'The leader of Islam was making his next war plan.'

This orientalist was basing his judgement only on conjecture, without taking into account the facts. But when we look at other traditions, it becomes clear what the Prophet was doing at that time. He was, in fact, making a plan to establish future peace. We know this from another tradition of the Prophet referring to the same war:

> 'God's angel came to him and said: "God has sent you a message of peace." On hearing this, Prophet Muhammad said, "God is peace, peace is from Him and peace returns to Him."'[3]

Prophet Muhammad's mission was spiritual purification of man. The Quran (2:129) calls it the purification of the soul, that is, making man a better human being.

Such an aim can be achieved only through counselling and persuasion. It is an aim that demands a re-engineering of the mind. This can be done only by awakening man's ability to think. The means of achieving this aim are not a political revolution, but rather an intellectual revolution.

That is why all the teachings of the Prophet are entirely based on the concept of peace. The Quran, as revealed to Prophet Muhammad, has more than 6000 verses. There are hardly forty verses in it which are about *qital* or war, that is, less than 1 per cent; whereas 99 per cent of the verses are designed to awaken man's intellectual faculties. We can say that the Quran is a book on the 'art of thinking'. It is in no way a treatise on the art of fighting.

The teachings of Prophet Muhammad and his exemplary way of living show that he not only projected the concept of peace, but that he was also able to develop a complete methodology of peaceful activism. The revolution he brought about was a practical one based on his ideology of peace.

The Philosophy of Patience

Patience, as a virtue, was given the utmost importance in the teachings of Prophet Muhammad. In the Quran, there are about 110 verses which contain the word 'patience' or *sabr*. The Quran, in fact, goes to the extent of saying that success depends upon patience alone:

> 'O People, be patient and steadfast, so that you may succeed.' (3:200)

It is this truth which is also expressed in the text of a long tradition of the Prophet:

'Learn that success goes with patience.'[4]

The tree of success always grows on the land of patience. History tells us that the majority of the world's pacifists have failed to achieve their aims, the commonest reason being that while they recognized the value of peace, they ignored the value of patience. Without exercising patience, it is impossible to launch a peace movement with any hope of success.

Generally, people who start peace movements first hold someone or some group to be their enemy, and then launch a movement against that enemy. For instance, Nelson Mandela and the African National Congress first spread hatred for the white settlers, and then declared that they were going to launch a peaceful movement to oust them from political power. The atmosphere of hostility thus created was the reason for the movement taking so long to achieve the desired result.

When peace activists launch an action against some group, it is vital that they have no negative feelings against its members. Else, they can never succeed in their peaceful mission. What usually happens is that when one group launches a peaceful movement against another group, it harbours a feeling of ill will towards its opponent. This feeling is caused by the perceived injustice committed by the other group.

This perception engenders hatred for the other party. This hatred gradually takes the form of violence, and if the desired success is not achieved through violence, this storm of hatred—boiling within the hearts of the group members—leads the group to engage in all kinds of destructive activities. Ultimately, to wipe out the enemy, they may even take to such extreme measures as wiping out themselves by resorting to suicide bombing.

Prophet Muhammad, like other reformers down the ages, also had to face all kinds of atrocities from his opponents, yet he never used the language of hatred against them. He even did his best to convince his companions that they should desist from nursing this feeling of hatred. We find abundant examples of this nature throughout his life.

For instance, in Makkah, the family of Yasir—a companion of the Prophet—was poor and weak, so the powerful opponents of the Prophet started beating them to compel them to leave the Prophet. On seeing this persecution, Prophet Muhammad did not utter a word against the opponents. He only exhorted Yasir and his family to exercise patience, because the reward for patience was Paradise. Prophet Muhammad was trying to drive home the point that they should refuse to be provoked, and under no circumstances harbour negative feelings against their opponents. The Quran, too, gives clear guidelines on this subject. It records the words of Prophet Abraham:

> 'We will, surely, bear with patience all the harm you do us.' (14:12)

By expressing its approval of Abraham's attitude, the Quran endorses the virtue of patience. Such patience is not an easy matter. It means adhering to positive thinking, despite acts of oppression by the other party.

Quiet Propagation

Prophet Muhammad continued to face injustice in his lifetime, but he always adhered strictly to the principle of patience and exhorted his companions to do likewise. Never in his meetings were the oppressive acts of the enemy discussed or even mentioned. Never did he heap verbal abuse on his oppressors. On the contrary, he had only good words for them. Never did he call his oppressors unbelievers (kafirs) or enemies. Rather, he always used the word *insan* (human being) for them. One ultimate example worth noting is that once when the Prophet's opponents had seriously injured him by stoning, he simply uttered these words:

'O God, guide my people for they do not know.'[5]

The way of undiluted, unilateral patience and benevolence adopted by the Prophet was intended to prevent feelings of hatred and grievance finding a place in his and his companions' hearts. A mind harbouring hatred and grievance is not competent to carry out the task of reform.

For many years after starting out on his mission in AD 610, Prophet Muhammad communicated his message quietly through private individual meetings. At that time, polytheism was in vogue in Makkah and in the whole of Arabia. The culture of polytheism dominated the lives of the Arabs, right from the moment of their birth till the day they died. In such a situation, introducing the message of monotheism was to simply invite confrontation.

This quiet propagation of the message of Islam was the first example of peaceful activism in the Prophet's life— a method he followed all his life. This principle of pacifism is expressed thus in the Quran:

'Good and evil deeds are not equal. Repel evil with what is better; then you will see that one who was once your enemy has become your dearest friend.' (41:34)

That is, if you face an enemy, do not allow yourselves to be influenced by the psychology of reaction and start retaliating; instead, solve the problem of enmity by following the peaceful method.

Prophet Muhammad continued to work peacefully, until eighty-three people had joined his mission. Then one of his senior companions, Abu Bakr, said to him that thenceforward they should work publicly. Prophet Muhammad answered:

'No, Abu Bakr, we are still only a very few.'6

Gradually, Prophet Muhammad's mission spread and the number of his followers increased. A time came when seventy-three people from Madinah came to meet him and confide in him that they had joined his mission. They said to him that he should no longer tolerate the oppression of the Makkans and that he should allow them to engage in jihad against them. Prophet Muhammad told them to go back, for he had not been commanded to wage war.

This action of the Prophet shows that he always acted with an eye on the consequences of his actions. He believed that our initiatives should always be aimed at yielding positive results—an initiative that proves counterproductive is no initiative at all.

To make a reasoned choice in favour of peaceful methods, it is vital that a man's mind should be free of feelings of hatred and revenge; he should be able to analyse events dispassionately. The importance of peaceful action can be understood only by a positive mind which plans its course of action in consonance with peaceful objectives.

Peaceful Thinking

Peace activism is ostensibly an external action, but it is the result of an internal awareness. It is a peaceful mind alone that can appreciate the benefits of peace activism and can properly bring it into play. Prophet Muhammad realized this truth. That is why, first and foremost, he worked towards building peace-loving minds. Only after he succeeded in this were he and his followers able to launch their movement, abiding by the principle of peace activism.

The Quran (2:129) calls this action of mind-building 'purification' (tazkia). It states that an important task of the Prophet was to work for the purification of minds, in other words, for the purification of the soul.

How does this purification work? We learn about it from a symbolic Hadith. In it the Prophet said that when a believer committed sin, his heart developed a black spot, but when he repented and sought forgiveness from God, his heart was cleansed of it. However, if he did not refrain from committing sins, the spots went on increasing, until they enveloped the whole heart.[7]

In this Hadith, Prophet Muhammad tells us of a very important truth which is borne out by a psychological study. This study tells us that when some thought comes to the human mind, it becomes embedded in the memory's storehouse, and is never expunged from it. The human mind comprises the conscious mind and the unconscious mind. When any thought enters the human mind, it first goes into the conscious mind and then gradually shifts to the unconscious one. This shifting process takes place mostly while we are sleeping. In this way, although a thought that is fresh in our memory today may be forgotten tomorrow, in reality, it is not lost, but becomes an integral part of our personality. In this way, our thoughts shape our personality.

The unpleasant events that life inevitably entails result in negative thoughts in our minds. These thoughts, if not immediately converted into positive ones, will eventually become part of our personality. It is the possessors of such negative personalities who become involved in war and violence against others. Violence is simply an external manifestation of a negative personality.

When any negative thought enters one's mind, one should immediately convert it into a positive feeling. A person who acts promptly to set in motion this process of mental conversion will build up a veritable storehouse of positive ideas in his unconscious mind. Only such people are truly capable of launching a movement for peace.

Prophet Muhammad understood this psychological reality and, through the purification of minds, formed a team of followers numbering more than one lakh who were staunchly committed to the principle of peace activism. While remaining strictly in a peaceful sphere, they were able—thanks to their positive way of thinking—to usher in a far-reaching and beneficent revolution.

7

Political Islam and
Its Proponents

A terrorist is not created in his mother's womb. It takes an environment of hatred—a whole jungle of hatred—to bring him into existence. The present-day community of Muslims has unfortunately provided such an environment. How did this jungle of hatred grow? For one, it has been cultivated by the extensive proliferation of a particular ideology among Muslims—a political interpretation of Islam, which offered Muslims the status of God's vicegerents on earth, with the right to rule the entire world on His behalf.

Islam was the leading civilization of the world in the period between the decline of ancient civilizations and the ascent of modern European ones. But ultimately, Western colonial powers established their dominance over the Muslim world; it was in reaction to this domination that political movements began to be launched in the name of Islam. The objective of these movements was to free Muslim countries from Western rule and to re-establish Muslim rule.

It was Syed Jamaluddin Afghani, born in Iran in 1838, who probably developed the concept of Islamic nationalism for the first time. During his lifetime, the colonial expansion of the West was at its peak and almost the entire Muslim world had, directly or indirectly, come under its rule. Jamaluddin Afghani made it his mission to bring down the colonial system and restore the political power of Muslim nations. Towards this end, he launched the movement known as pan-Islamism. It aimed at bringing together the Muslims of the entire world to form a united international power, which would defeat Western nations and set the Muslim world free from their clutches.

Jamaluddin Afghani failed to achieve his political target, but what he did successfully was to sow the seeds of hatred for Western nations in Muslim minds all over the world. As a result, Muslims in general came to regard Western nations as their enemies. Almost all the Muslim leaders of his time began to think in negative and political terms. The more prominent of these were Sayyid Qutb and Amir Shakib Arsalan in the Arab world, Muhammad Iqbal and Sayyed Abul Ala Maududi in the Indian subcontinent, and later Ayatollah Khomeini in Iran.

Initially, the movement focused on the expulsion of Western forces from the Muslim world. More appropriately, it was an initiative to gain political freedom. Thus, in the times of Afghani, this movement was more political than religious in nature, with its slogan being 'The East for Easterners'.

After Afghani, this revolutionary movement entered another phase. Now it was given an ideological form. The movement, which had been described in communal terms (with reference to the global Muslim community), was now given an Islamic hue. An attempt was made to Islamize their communal thinking by developing a complete ideology based on the political interpretation of Islam. If earlier the thinking had been that the Western nations were usurpers and that a restitution of Muslims' political rights must be demanded from them, in the next phase ideologists developed the theory that Islam had a system covering the whole of human life and that this included politics. The Muslims were, therefore, duty-bound to capture political power by force so that Islam might be implemented as a total system. The promoters of this movement held that so long as Islam was not adopted by the believers in toto, as a complete system, their faith would not be acceptable to God. It followed that bringing about a political revolution became a binding obligation, like prayers and fasting.

In this second phase, two Muslim leaders figured most prominently: the Egyptian intellectual Sayyid Qutb (d. 1966) and Sayyed Abul Ala Maududi (d. 1979), a Muslim ideologue from the Indian subcontinent. Both these leaders found themselves in a very favourable environment—an environment that now made it possible for their books to be translated into many languages and thus for their ideas to spread over almost the entire Muslim world. As a consequence, Muslims in almost all parts of the globe were directly influenced by their political ideology. Some became actively involved, while the thinking of others, shaped by this ideology, centred on political Islam. All dreamed of the political glory of Islam.

This movement, designed to establish political Islam, gave rise to various other movements. Two of these movements grew into prominence: Al Ikhwan al-Muslimun, or the Muslim Brotherhood, established in 1928 in the Arab world, and the Jamat-e-Islami established in 1941 on the subcontinent. Both were highly organized movements and subsequently launched campaigns to establish Islamic rule in Muslim countries such as Egypt, Sudan, Pakistan, Afghanistan, Algeria, Tunisia and Malaysia.

At first, these movements sought to establish Muslim rule by spreading their ideology of political Islam. When they failed on this score, they started taking part in the national elections in the countries where they were active. When they failed on this front too, they resorted to militancy.

This political movement of the Muslims intensified in the latter half of the twentieth century. It was during these days that the Jews established their rule in Palestine in the name of Israel. Now Muslims believe that the Jews are rejected by God, while the Muslims themselves are the chosen people. So, finding the dominance of the Jews over the Muslims intolerable, they made a frantic bid to obliterate the Jews from the face of the earth. The pro-Islam movement of the first half of the twentieth century ultimately turned into an anti-Jewish movement in the second half of the century.

Events have demonstrated that, in spite of making every conceivable effort, Muslims have failed in their campaign against the Jews. On every front, right from the United Nations to the Aqsa Mosque of Jerusalem, they have had total defeat inflicted upon them. It is the ensuing build-up of a defeatist mentality which has culminated perforce in the phenomenon of 'Islamic terrorism'.

Though ostensibly aimed at re-establishing Islamic rule, the political Islam movement actually grew as a political reaction to the circumstances in which Muslims found themselves at that particular point in time. Its inspiration and its impact were totally negative. The movement was the result of anti-Western rather than pro-Islam feelings, and for precisely this reason it rapidly turned violent.

According to Islam, a truly Islamic movement arises out of feelings of benevolence for all of humanity. Its target being neither land nor power, it is always carried out through peaceful means. It never adopts violence. If Muslim movements of the modern age opted for the way of extremism, it was because they were not genuinely Islamic in nature. The truth is that these Muslim social movements, which had only the community agenda in mind, adopted the name of Islam purely as a means of self-justification.

If you read the Quran, nowhere in it will you find any mention of 'political Islam'. The Quran contains neither information nor injunctions which could lead to the setting up of a political system.

The eighteenth-century French thinker Rousseau, who was greatly concerned with the human condition, wrote a treatise called *The Social Contract* (1762). He opened his book with this arresting statement: 'Man is born free; and everywhere he is in chains.'

This is the language of a political book, a book which was to contribute to the ideas and policies of the leaders of the French Revolution and which ultimately gained worldwide currency. But if you read the Quran, you will see that it begins not with a diatribe against human inequality with its implied criticism of wrong governance, but simply with praises of God. And it ends with the necessity to seek refuge in God against Satan. In the Quran and the Hadith, there is no mention of the system of state. Nor is there any mention of revolt against any existing system. Neither is there any indication as to how a political ruler or *khalifah* is to be appointed or selected. No such principles are set forth in Islam, neither from an ideological nor from a practical point of view. In short, it is clear that no aspect of political Islam is dealt with anywhere in the Quran and the Hadith.

At more than one place in the Quran we are told what the Prophet's tasks were in accordance with the divine plan. These were recitation of the verses of the Quran; purification of man; teaching of the scriptures; and teaching of wisdom. In none of the verses are we told that the task of the Prophet was to establish Islamic rule in the world. Such verses of the Quran as presented by the champions of political Islam in support of their cause were distorted to serve their own ends. The truth is that giving a political interpretation to Islam is a despicable act and in no way serves the higher aims of the religion.

8

The Muslim Brotherhood

The Muslim Brotherhood (Al Ikhwan al-Muslimun), more than any other individual or organization, must be held responsible for the development of anti-Western thinking in the Arab world in the twentieth century, which has culminated in the culture of hatred, violence and suicide bombing. This organization was ostensibly formed in the name of religion but, in its present reality, it is a political movement given to violent actions. It is the spread of its ideology that is responsible for the negative mentality of the entire present-day generation of Arabs; it is no exaggeration to say that the majority of the Arabs of this generation directly or indirectly have become supporters of the Muslim Brotherhood.

The Muslim Brotherhood was founded in 1928 in the Egyptian city of Ismailia, where Hassan al Banna, the founder of this organization, was a schoolteacher. Ismailia was and is an administration centre of the Suez Canal. Al Banna was appalled by the many conspicuous signs of foreign military and economic domination in Ismailia: the British military camps, the public utilities owned by foreign firms and the luxurious residences of the foreign employees of the Suez Canal Company, next to the squalid dwellings of the Egyptian workers.[1] It was this that impelled Hassan al Banna to found the Muslim Brotherhood in 1928.

The traditional outlook of the age that gave birth to the movement no doubt accounts for it having adopted a religious framework, though its actual motive was political. Its principal objective was to purify Egypt and the entire Arab world of the political infiltration of the West, and it initially arose in the spirit of serving the Muslim cause. But when its promoters found that they could not achieve their objective through peaceful means, they opted for violence against their supposed enemies. When even violent activities failed to achieve their ends, they finally resorted to suicide bombing, as if now their slogan had become 'If we cannot put an end to you, we will put an end to ourselves.'

A number of Muslim extremists met with such leaders like Abdul Wahhab Azzam and Sayyed Qutb, who were the leading lights of the Muslim Brotherhood. This extremist organization exerted such a powerful influence that the thinking of large numbers of people was entirely shaped by members of the Muslim Brotherhood and their literature and ideals. All those who are associated with this movement are either violent in theory (that is, they believe in the violent ideology, but are not practically involved) or violent in practice. Osama bin Laden is an extreme case of the latter phenomenon.

It is common practice among the members of the Muslim Brotherhood to concoct false interpretations of the Quran and the Hadith to justify their extremist political views. In their formative years, many young Muslims are not in a position to separate the wrong from the right. They do not appreciate the difference between fiery speeches and logical statements. They do not know the difference between an emotional move and a realistic one. That is why their thinking often runs on the same lines as the Brotherhood's philosophy until their minds become fully conditioned in the extremist mould.

A number of incidents which took place subsequently contributed to a consolidation of the extremists' viewpoints, for instance, Israel's attack on Egypt, Jordan and Syria in 1967 and the consequent expansion of its territory; the Russian army's invasion of Afghanistan in 1979; America's attack on Afghanistan; and America's continuing patronage of Israel. All these incidents helped assert the Muslims' negative stereotyping of the West. All through this period, there was no one who could de-condition their minds and enable the Muslims to think objectively. As a result, they threw themselves into a violent jihad against the West.

If you visit the Arab world today and talk to the Arabs, you will find that most of them regard not only the Jews but also the Americans as their enemies; indeed, they regard America as the number one enemy of Islam. This negative thinking has been fostered among Arabs entirely by the Muslim Brotherhood. The Palestinian issue and the Palestinian youths have also played a role in the emergence of such thinking, for the Palestinian youths joined the Muslim Brotherhood in large numbers and converted it into a militant organization.

Those conversant with Arab history know that for the

last thousand years Palestine has served as the centre of the Arab political and national movement. For the Arabs, Palestine is such an emotional issue that the mere mention of it sends them into a kind of frenzy. There are few Arabs who can think dispassionately on this subject.

Palestine assumed importance for the Arabs during the life of the Prophet himself while he was still in Makkah, following his spiritual journey (isra), which has been recorded in the Quran:

'Holy is He who took His servant by night from the sacred place of worship [at Makkah] to the remote house of worship [at Jerusalem]—the precincts of which We have blessed.' (17:1)

The Muslim interpretation of the mystical journey of the Prophet from Makkah to Jerusalem led them to believe that it was their right to rule over Palestine, though there is no statement made to this effect either in the Quran or in the Hadith. On the contrary, it is clearly laid down in the Quran that God said to the Jews through Prophet Moses:

'O my people, enter the Holy Land which God has assigned for you.' (5:21)

Palestine came under Muslim rule during the time of Caliph Umar, the second caliph. The possession of this land by Muslims was acceptable neither to the Christians nor to the Jews, for Palestine was a sacred place for both these religious groups. Therefore, anger against the Muslims continued to simmer. This culminated in the protracted war known as the Crusades. Throughout this long-drawn-out war, which was waged intermittently from 1095 to 1291, the Christian rulers of Europe united themselves in the fight against the Muslims, but they were ultimately defeated by Salahuddin Ayyubi or Saladin (d. 1193), who demonstrated extraordinary military prowess. Consequently, Salahuddin Ayyubi became the greatest hero of all the Arabs. In the following centuries, Palestine underwent many vicissitudes and, finally, in 1948, its history took a turn for the worse, with large parts of its territory being restored to the Jews with the support of the Christians. The Jews are still Palestine's rulers.

Today, the entire Arab world is dreaming of the return of the era of Salahuddin Ayyubi, about whom Arabic literature is full of stories of epic dimensions. The following couplet by an Arab poet, Az Zarkali, is the watchword of all Arabs: 'Let us bring Salahuddin back and revive the historic day of Hitteen.'

This was the psychological environment that gave rise to bin Laden. Therefore, it was but natural that he soon began to be seen as another Salahuddin. All the lofty perceptions people had of Salahuddin came to be associated with bin Laden. If it was the Muslim Brotherhood which formed his violent mentality, it was the historical traditions of Salahuddin which accorded to him the status of a much-admired Muslim hero.

9

Political Extremism and Islam

The Quran teaches us not be extremist in our religion. Its exact words are:

'People of the Book! Do not go to extremes in your religion.' (4:171)

We also learn from a saying of Prophet Muhammad that extremist tendencies have always been the chief reason for religious groups going astray. That is why the Prophet once observed:

'Sedulously refrain from extremism, for previous communities were destroyed only because of their extremist tendencies in religious matters.'[1]

Ghulu, meaning extremism, is engendered in a religious community when it goes into a state of decline, and is, in fact, a sign of its degeneration. There is a tradition of Prophet Muhammad which forewarns his followers of the rot that can set in. He said that all those evils which had arisen in previous communities would also arise, but on a greater scale, in his own community. To make his meaning clear, he said:

'Where previous communities were divided into 72 sects, Muslims will be divided into 73 sects.'[2]

There are innumerable cases of ideological extremism in Islamic history. But we also find among Muslims another kind of extremism which probably never existed in previous communities. When the Prophet said that while the Israelites were divided into seventy-two sects and the Muslims would be divided into seventy-three sects, he was giving an example of this other kind of ghulu (extremism) which can be described as political extremism. No previous community had ever been crowned by such political glory as was enjoyed by the Muslims for almost a thousand years after the emergence of Islam. Political glory was not, however, a part of the Islamic creed, but a part of history. But Muslims stressed this fact of political glory to such an extent that, for all intents and purposes, it became incorporated in their religious creed. The result of this political extremism is the violent jihad we experience in the Muslim world of today.

Ultimately, extremist concepts such as 'Muslims are God's vicegerents on earth and, as such, they have the right to rule over other communities' were developed. Religion came to be regarded as synonymous with a complete state, and a religion of this nature could not be fully observed unless it was established as the basis and framework of the state. Those promoting these ideologies and politicizing Islam believed that Muslims were a superior community, with the right to treat other communities as inferior. As a result, to this day, Muslims find it difficult to tolerate any sort of dominance. They believe that their religious obligations can never be fully discharged just by performing prayers and observing fasting. They imagine it is incumbent upon them to strive to establish divine rule on earth.

A set of beliefs such as these has nothing to do with the religion as revealed by God. It is nothing but a case of political extremism. But present-day Muslims are largely under the influence of this extremist way of thinking—some consciously, others unconsciously.

Muhammad, the Prophet of Islam, achieved considerable political success while he was still alive; and this was built on rapidly by his successors, the caliphs. Unfortunately, along with success comes the opportunity to abuse it. That is why, according to the Hadith, the Muslims were divided, in terms of ideological extremism, into seventy-two sects, while the seventy-third sect was concerned with political extremism. Of course, the evil of ideological extremism is found as much in Muslim as in other communities, but it is the former's bent of political extremism that has aggravated this issue further.

Congregations led by earlier prophets did not achieve political success during their prophets' lifetimes. Their prophets only left them an ideological legacy. That is why we find political extremism absent in them. At the most, they can indulge only in ideological extremism.

According to the Quran (22:78) and the Hadith, the greatest duty of the Muslim community—*shahadat 'alan naas*—is to spread the divine message of Islam peacefully among other nations. But because of their extremist political approach, present-day Muslims have abandoned this missionary duty. The most dangerous aspect of their forsaking this duty is their labelling of non-missionary activities as missionary work. For instance, debates, political protests, Muslim-reform activities, community work, are all termed missionary work by today's Muslims.

The most urgent task today is to inculcate this consciousness of the mission and to set up an educational system on the principles of this mission. Muslims should be raised as a missionary group—or witnesses (22:78) as it is called in the Quran—and should be prevented from indulging in non-missionary activities. Without taking such a step, missionary work cannot be effectively performed.

The Quran (5:67) tells us that the secret of protection from enemy plots lies in the performance of dawah. That is, if Muslims engage in dawah work, their lives, properties and wealth will be protected by God. In short, the communication of the religious message is the responsibility of Muslims, while the protection of their worldly interests rests with God.

According to a famous tradition, 'our actions are judged by our intentions'.[3] Intention here is the equivalent of what is generally called spirit. This means that although there are many actions which in form appear to be morally acceptable, it is to the spirit of these acts rather than their external form that Islam attaches real importance.

From a Hadith we learn that Prophet Muhammad, speaking of the Muslims of the future, predicted that only the external form of Islamic actions would survive.[4] That is to say, the actions of the Muslims of the future would be lacking in internal spirit, and only the outer form of their religious observances would persist. People will remain ignorant of the true spirit of Islam so long as they are conversant only with its forms and attach importance only to the externals.

It is easy to understand how extremism or ghulu stems from this flawed perception. In the early days of Islam, the spirit was alive, and was accorded full attention. But when in later generations degeneration set in, external rituals began to be given more importance. This is a frequent occurrence.

Let me explain this with an example from the world of business. The phrase 'customer-friendly behaviour' is often used in business jargon. It means if a businessman is to be successful, he must appear to be friendly to his customers. Now let us compare this with behaviour in the family. You will not hear any parents say that their behaviour towards their children is 'child-friendly'. The reason for this difference is that the spirit of love for their children wells up naturally in parents, and so they do not need to talk about it or make a display of it.

The case of a businessman is totally different. A businessman has no love or compassion for his customers.

It is solely the desire for commercial gain that inspires him to make a display of these qualities. It is human nature that wherever the internal spirit is alive, no importance will be attached to the externals, while in the absence of spirit, the maximum attention will be paid to formal etiquette.

This is the human mentality that produces the phenomenon called ghulu. It is a fact that ghulu, or extremism, is invariably relevant to externals and not to internal realities.

When we look at the Muslims of today, we find that the prediction of the Prophet has come true. One kind of ghulu that has developed among Muslims is the one pertaining to ideology, for instance, the concept of spiritual leaders being intermediaries between God and man, and the concept of sacredness of graves.

Today, violent activities are going on in the name of jihad all over the world. There are some who are directly involved, while others justify these acts in their speeches and writings. A third group consists of those who are silent. But according to the shariah principle, they too are involved, for silence is not enough—it is their duty to publicly condemn such un-Islamic acts.

This political ghulu is the greatest weakness of Muslims; it has overridden all the human qualities that qualify a community for a position of honour and glory—qualities such as benevolence, universality of approach (that is, looking at all human beings as God's family), positive thinking, keeping abreast of the changing times, thinking realistically, acknowledgement of others, fostering the dawah spirit, giving importance to the value of peace, and objective thinking.

The greatest harm done by political extremism is that it deters Muslims from emerging from the shell of the past. This is the cause of their failure to understand the present. In the past, war was something which decided the fate of communities. But in modern times, peaceful resources have become much more powerful. Yet, Muslims seem unaware of these resources. In the past, the economy was based on agriculture. Now it is based on industry. Electronic communications just did not exist in the past, whereas today, communications have become one of the greatest strengths of mankind. But Muslims are blissfully unaware of all these developments. That is why they have not been able to take advantage of the blessings of the modern age. Moreover, in the past, all resources were in the hands of the king, but today is the age of institutions. It has become possible in modern times for any community which so desires to build up a parallel empire by establishing institutions.

The violent jihad, prevalent in modern times, dates back to Tipu Sultan (d. 1799). This has been a 200-year-long jihad without any positive result, and with no real movement directed as yet at reassessment of values, aims or objectives. The reason lies in the Muslims' lack of awareness. Today, the greatest task is to remedy this shortcoming, without which there is no possibility of any positive change.

About seventy years ago, Amir Shakib Arsalan published a book titled *Our Decline: Its Causes and Remedies*. The author concluded that the reason for Muslim backwardness lay in abandoning jihad. He quoted an Arabic couplet in support:

'I refrained from taking part in war, so that I might live. But I did not find in it life. Life was for those who went ahead and waged the war.'[5]

This point has been made repeatedly by Muslim leaders over the last two centuries. The result has been that this militant ideology has spread among Muslims all over the world. The jihadi model has become the sole inspiration for action. But when we take stock of the outcome, we find that this has proved to be counterproductive. In such a situation, it would be more appropriate to modify the couplet and say:

'I adopted the path of war for life and survival, but finally I learnt that life and survival are only for those who abandon the militant course in favour of a peaceful course of action.'

10

Analysing the Phenomenon of Terrorism

Those who launch political or religious movements aimed at revolution or reform generally fall into two categories. In the first are those who promote their own ideas, such as Karl Marx, who formulated an ideology (later known as communism) which was the product of his own original thinking. Now, if Marx's ideology, or the movement launched by him, is to be upheld or discarded, it can only be done on the basis of an independent analysis of his writings. Since Marx's ideology bears very little relation to any other contemporary or earlier philosophy or economic theory, it is irrelevant to make comparisons between it and the ideas to be found in the works of other profound thinkers on the human condition.

On the other hand there are those, in the second category, who do not formulate any ideology of their own, but who invoke the authority of some existing religion or philosophy to give a veneer of respectability to their movements. Into this category falls Osama bin Laden and his supporters. Making no claim to having produced an ideology of his own, he proclaims that it is in obedience to the teachings of Islam that he has risen to wage jihad against its enemies. He defines his goal as the imposition of the commandments of Islam, and insists that everything he does towards this end, including acts of extreme violence, is governed by Islam—of which he sedulously portrays himself as a representative.

Now, in choosing to describe his violent activities as 'Islamic jihad', a Muslim terrorist has himself given us a definite criterion by which to judge the tenability of his stand. This terminology, in being demonstrably erroneous (the precise meaning can be ascertained from the Quran), provides a yardstick by which to form an accurate opinion of his personal credibility. This so-called Islamic aspect of bin Laden's movement is pertinent to any assessment of his actions, in that it enables the analyst to pinpoint a known and established criterion in the light of which his stand or ideology may be judged, be it right or wrong. In other words, it is possible in this case to give a verdict which even bin Laden and his ilk cannot, in principle, refute.

Furthermore, the criterion of Islam projected by terrorists like bin Laden—by which he himself may be judged—is not something vague or shadowy or controversial. The Quran, the holy book which has enshrined the tenets of Islam for all time to come, still exists in its pristine form and is quite unequivocal in its exposition of moral precepts. Similarly, the traditions of the Prophet are also fully preserved in the books of traditions, and just by studying them we can learn, without so much as an iota of doubt, about the path which the Prophet of Islam expected his followers to tread. Moreover, from these sources we can distinguish between those whose actions are in accordance with this model and those whose conduct goes against it.

Speaking of Prophet Muhammad, a certain Western scholar has very aptly observed:

'Muhammad was born within the full light of history.'[1]

When the Prophet of Islam, Muhammad ibn Abdullah, came to the world, paper and writing were already in use, so it was possible to keep a full record of his life and teachings. The books recording them have been translated into a number of different languages and are widely available across the world. Muhammad's life is thus an open book and is as well known as the life of any other historical figure. There are, therefore, ample opportunities to learn about the example set by the Prophet of Islam. There is no textual scope for Muslim extremists to make wilful distortions of the Islamic ideal.

Even more important is the fact that Islam as a religion has been fully recorded in the annals of history. Everything regarding Islam is known and established. The Quran, Islam's most sacred book, consists of about 6500 verses which are couched in a language that is clear and lucid. Nothing in the Quran is ambiguous. This being so, it is possible to learn the message of the Quran simply by reading it.

Islamic scholars have, moreover, devised principles which enable us to distinguish between correct and distorted versions of Islamic ideology. Distinguishing the right interpretation of Islam from distortions of it and distinguishing the truth about Prophet Muhammad from accounts misrepresenting his life and achievements are therefore as easy and straightforward as separating white seeds from black ones. This is an extremely important point, for it means that, based on bona fide sources, an analysis of the actions of bin Laden and his ilk is both practically possible and trustworthy.

Keeping all of the above facts in mind, we will examine in the next few chapters those aspects of Islam which are relevant to the movement launched and perpetuated by Osama bin Laden and his supporters. We shall, moreover, place this analysis in a sharper perspective by clearly defining the genuine teachings of Islam and see whether these teachings negate or validate their actions.

11

Countering the Terrorists' Ideology

The most important point in understanding terrorism is that it cannot be eliminated by bombs and guns. It is not a question of gun versus gun, but rather of gun versus ideology. Terrorism stands by an ideology, and to discredit and abolish that ideology, one needs a powerful counter-ideology. Without this, it is just not possible to rid the world of the menace of terrorism.

America had to face the spectre of communism in the twentieth century, for, with the formation of the Soviet Union, communism had come to wield overwhelming political power. But America did not attempt to bring down the communist empire by attacking the USSR, in the way that it later attacked Afghanistan and Iraq to put an end to the Islamic jihad movement. How then did the communist empire disintegrate without any military onslaught? The answer is that America waged a large-scale ideological battle against communism, which included disseminating anti-communist literature throughout the world. This cast serious doubts upon the validity of the communist ideology. One good example of this strategy was the way the book

New Class by Milovan Djilas was introduced to the readers by the *Reader's Digest* under the heading 'The Book that is Shaking the Communist World'.[1]

Similarly, if the world is to be rid of terrorism, its underpinning ideology will have to be proved wrong by the kind of literature which will give forceful arguments against it, making it clear to the public that Islamists are the problem, and not the solution to the problem, that terrorist vendors are a menace and not a blessing, and that the path they show leads to hell, not to heaven.

Towards this end, we shall, first of all, have to understand the ideological bases of today's terrorism. And then we shall have to demolish these ideological bases by means of a counter-ideology. We shall have to impress upon the adherents of terrorism that what they want to achieve through violence can be achieved in a far better way by peaceful means.

Moreover, we shall have to remind them that the present world is one of challenge and competition, and that is why differences are unavoidable. It has to be emphasized that the solution to these differences does not lie in obliterating them, but rather in learning the art of difference management.

They must, likewise, be convinced that the war they are waging is, in fact, not aimed at some supposed enemy, but is rather against the law of nature itself. And who has the power to fight the law of nature and succeed?

Whenever anyone launches himself on a course of action, it is the result of his first having formed an opinion on the rights and wrongs of the given situation. Therefore, for a counter-ideology to be effective, it should make those at whom it is aimed take a step back and reassess their objectives and modus operandi. If their thinking is changed, their actions will automatically follow suit. Today, people's thinking is marred by extremism and they therefore act accordingly. If people's thinking could be turned in a peaceful direction, their actions would never be violent and disruptive. This should be the sole aim of such an ideological encounter.

As is recorded in the annals of history, the Arabs ruled the region of Spain called Andalusia for about 800 years. Monuments of Arab rule may still be seen in many towns such as Seville, Cordoba and Granada. These are regularly visited by large numbers of Arab tourists, as they remind them of the feats performed by their ancestors. To the Arabs, the Spain of old is a sign of past pride.

Writings on the subject, by both Arab and non-Arab Muslims, are steeped in nostalgia for a bygone era. After reading a number of such works, which lamented the end of Arab rule in Spain, I had the opportunity to visit Spain twice, in November 1994 and in December 2003. On both these visits, I toured different parts of Spain. The impressions I formed were totally different from what I had read. On the one hand, I saw edifices or the ruins of edifices of the Muslim period, and on the other, I saw the modern, well-developed cities of Spain. There were a great number of beautiful constructions, and modern amenities were available everywhere.

These two vistas produced within me a feeling of thankfulness rather than of grief or nostalgia. I saw old Spain and modern Spain as the stages in the historic journey of man. I felt that the caravan of humanity had passed the earlier, traditional age and entered the modern, scientific age. I looked at the advanced civilization of modern Spain. My heart was filled with feelings of gratitude to the Creator.

During my journey in Spain, I wrote a travelogue (later published in book form), one paragraph of which was published in the monthly *Al-Risala*. The gist of it is that instead of feeling regret for what is now lost, present-day Muslims should rather acknowledge the achievements of the Spanish people. They should realize that while they, the Muslims, had led humanity forward through the traditional age, the Spanish people had, by their unstinting efforts, led their country into the scientific age. They had thus succeeded for the first time in their history in building a beautiful world for themselves. These thoughts came to me while I was walking through Madrid's splendid new airport. The emotions brought by these thoughts made tears well up in my eyes. I finished the paragraph by exhorting my readers: 'Come! Let us thank God so that we may be found deserving of being admitted to the much better world of God, that is, Paradise. In this world God has arranged only a glimpse of Paradise as an advance introduction to the far better world to come.'[2]

The greatest weakness of many present-day Muslims is that their concept of history is totally governed by their restricted world view. They look at history from the Muslim point of view rather than from the human viewpoint. It is this way of thinking that poses the greatest problem to present-day Muslims. Thousands of articles on Palestine and Israel have been published in Urdu, Arabic, Persian and English. Without exception, they emphasize the oppression of the Palestinians by the Jews. Indeed, nothing positive about the Jews is ever mentioned in Muslim writings.

I travelled to Israel and Palestine on three occasions—in August 1995, in October 1997 and in October 2008. My observations during these visits were totally different from what I had read in Muslim writings. This showed that the Muslims were giving an entirely one-sided, thus unjust and biased, picture. They forgot that the Quran says:

'Woe to the unjust.' (83:1)

One aspect of the conflict between the Arabs and the Jews, affecting both Palestine and Israel, which is never fully taken account of, is the Arabs' determination to continue their militant activities, unmindful of the consequences in which they themselves emerge as the greater sufferers. This is why the Arab settlements in Palestine bear witness to destruction, while the Jewish areas are characterized by verdant stretches of fields and gardens—a different picture altogether. Israel has the most modern infrastructure and everyone has access to the best educational facilities. Even the Arabs who live there peacefully are in a better condition than in many Muslim countries.

The concept of the greater religious community or ummah dominates the mindset of present-day Muslims. Their sole concern now is their own community and they are indifferent to the rest of humanity. Their thinking is totally Muslim-oriented; they look at every issue from the Muslim point of view and all their speeches and writings focus on Muslim problems. Problems relating to general humanity are of no interest to them. They neither think about others nor do they do anything for them.

'Islamists', especially the suicide bombers, are the product of this negative thinking. They fail to see any evil in Muslims and, at the same time, cannot see any good in non-Muslims. They are friends of their own community alone and the enemies of all other communities. The Quran calls God 'Lord of the Worlds', but the 'Islamists' have made God 'Lord of the Muslims'. The Quran says of Prophet Muhammad that he is a 'mercy to all mankind' (21:107), but these have turned Prophet Muhammad into a 'mercy to Muslims' only.

By wrongly interpreting the Quran, the 'Islamists' have created their own radical version of Islam. According to this version, hating non-believers will be rewarded as if this were a form of worship, while killing them will be a guarantee of entry into Paradise.

Terrorism is undoubtedly a violent movement directed against all of humanity. However, to put an end to this movement—instead of repaying its adherents in the same token of violence—what is required is to de-condition them by meeting them on an intellectual level and impressing upon them the true and positive picture of Islam. Without producing an effective counter-ideology to it, there can be no hope of stemming the tide of terrorism.

12

Does the Quran Support Terrorism?

Some persons claiming to be true Muslims have devised their own ideological base in favour of an armed struggle. To lend credence to their ideas, they have wrongly interpreted certain verses from the Quran. They have done this without citing any of the established Islamic religious authorities. Here, we shall analyse some of those verses to show the untenability of their pro-violence ideology.

One of the arguments to support their ideas is derived from the verse which says that God's religion was completed only with the revelations sent to Prophet Muhammad. Since there are both individual and social commands in Islam, the proponents of political Islam seek a total enforcement of the religion and hold this necessary for Muslims to secure political power; they argue that it is only with political power that Islam can be enforced in its totality throughout the world. This forcible taking over of the reins of political power seems as essential to them as believing in the veracity of Islam.

The verse in question regarding the theory of a complete religion is as follows:

'Today I have completed your religion for you.' (5:3)

The command of Islam derived from this verse by ideologues of political Islam is not taken directly from the wording of the text. According to their interpretation, this verse should have read as follows: 'Today I have completed the Divine Religion for you', that is, the religion revealed from time to time, right from the time of Adam to Jesus, has now finally been completed with the revelations made to Muhammad ibn Abdullah.

But the actual wording of the verse is different and is as follows: 'Today I have completed your religion for you.' As we learn from the traditions of the Prophet, this was the verse of the Quran to be revealed last. (Most of the verses of the Quran were revealed to fit particular situations or occasions. Later, at the time of compilation, these verses were arranged in the form of chapters, but their arrangement does not follow the chronological order of revelation.)

This clearly indicates that the completion of religion means the completion of the religion revealed to Muhammad. This verse is thus a declaration that the last and final verse of the Quran had been revealed and that no other verse or chapter would be revealed in future. This verse shows the completion of the Quranic revelation rather than the completeness of divine religion.

Some have deduced from this verse the theory that there is an evolutionary gradualness in God's religion, that is, only elementary commands had been revealed to the earlier prophets and subsequently more commands continued to be revealed to the succeeding prophets. So no previous prophet was given the complete religion. The complete religion was revealed only to the final prophet, Prophet Muhammad, son of Abdullah. Therefore, they conclude that Islam is a complete religion, while the previous prophets were recipients of an incomplete religion.

This theory is entirely baseless. We learn from the Quran (42:13) that God's religion is one single religion, which was revealed equally to all the prophets. Moreover, the Quran states:

'We make no distinction between any of God's messengers.' (2:285)

The Quran expressly asserts that all the prophets were guided in the complete sense and that Prophet Muhammad was asked by God to follow the previous prophets:

'They are those whom God guided aright, so you follow their guidance.' (6:90)

Now if the religion given to Prophet Muhammad was a complete religion, while the religion given to the previous prophets was an incomplete one, then this verse of the Quran would make no sense. It is almost inconceivable that the perfect Prophet would be commanded to follow prophets whose knowledge of religion was incomplete.

Again, with reference to the verse on the completeness of religion, it is argued that only elementary commands were revealed to earlier prophets—commands relating solely to things like belief and worship, and not to social or political life. That is why, the argument goes, the need to establish political power did not arise with regard to the teachings of the previous religions.

The ideologues of political Islam hold that as Islam is a complete religion containing individual as well as social commands, political power is necessary, for without it Islam can never be implemented in its entirety.

This theory too is totally baseless. According to the Quran, the previous prophets were given the same religion as was given to the Prophet of Islam. The Bible still contains the shariah (laws) relating to social matters as revealed to Prophet Moses.

The truth is that the religion of all the prophets was governed by the principle that no individual should be obliged to follow that part of God's religion which was beyond his capacity to do so. The same rule held good for society too.

As per this precept, in any given situation, one will be held accountable only for whatever part of the religion it is possible to follow and not for those other parts, the undertaking of which is ruled out by circumstances. For instance, if one does not have sufficient means, the obligation to give in charity (zakat) will not be applicable. Furthermore, under no circumstances is a person or group authorized to engage in violence in order that all the divine commands may be fully enforced.

Now let us look at verse 13, chapter 42 of the Quran, which reads:

'God has ordained for you the same religion which he enjoined on Noah, and which We have revealed to you, and which We enjoined upon Abraham and Moses and Jesus, so that you should remain steadfast in religion and not become divided in it. What you call upon the polytheists to do is hard for them; God chooses for Himself whoever He pleases and guides towards Himself those who turn to Him.'

With reference to this verse, the argument put forward is that here religion (ad-Din) means God's complete religion, that is, the believers have been commanded in this verse to enforce it in its totality—which would mean all aspects of religion, including beliefs, worship, laws, moral values—without any dilution or subtraction of any of its parts.

The extremists hold the view that since a total system of this kind cannot be enforced without political power, it is essential for Muslims to make every effort to capture that power.

This kind of ideology has nothing to do with the verse concerned. Its argument is entirely based on the Arabic word aqimu, which has been taken to mean 'enforce' and given a clearly political connotation. However, aqimu means to 'follow' or to 'observe'. This verse simply means that God's religion is a universal religion; therefore, accept it with your heart and your soul and adopt it fully in your life. According to the commentators of the Quran, all that the religion specifically connotes is monotheism (that is, worshipping the one and only God), honesty, sincerity, truthfulness, compassion, and the cultivation of other such virtues.

A similar point has been made in the Quran:

'Be strict in observing justice.' (4:135)

Although this verse literally means to adhere unswervingly to justice, it has been wilfully misinterpreted to give it a political connotation. But all this verse aims to do is impart sterling values which will improve the moral character of the individual. That is, it advocates that every individual Muslim should always follow the principle of justice in his personal life. This verse implies submission and yielding to God's Will by every believer in all his actions, but it has been wrongly given a political connotation that Muslims are duty-bound to enforce their system of justice upon others everywhere in order to raise the standard of Islam all over the world.

One of the sources of the concept of Islam as a ruling system is the word 'command' or *hukm* as it occurs in the Quran (6:57); this word is taken in the political sense and then it is claimed that the task of the Prophet was to exterminate the 'enemy' (*taghoot*) and enforce divine rule globally. This interpretation of the word 'enemy' is totally baseless. This word is used in the Quran in the metaphysical rather than in the political sense.

Another such verse appears in chapter 12 of the Quran. It records the conversation of Prophet Joseph with his companion in prison, in the course of which he said:

'The command is for none but God.' (12:40)

The ideologues of political Islam take this verse to mean that political power on earth is the sole prerogative of God and that Prophet Joseph's mission was to establish a political system in the land of Egypt in which political sovereignty belonged to God alone. This is a baseless interpretation of the Quran. Placing Prophet Joseph's conversation correctly back in the context of the verse, it is a rejection of idol worship and the enjoining of a God-oriented life. This is borne out by the following excerpt from the same chapter:

'All those you worship instead of Him are mere names you and your fathers have invented.' (12:40)

Moreover, the very actions of Prophet Joseph totally negate the interpretation of the political ideologues. As the Quran tells us, during the lifetime of Prophet Joseph, Egypt was ruled by an idolatrous king. Prophet Joseph never challenged his power, but rather, acknowledging his sovereignty, accepted a post in his government (which today would be the equivalent of minister of food and supplies). This act on the part of Prophet Joseph clearly shows that he used the words 'the command is for none but God' in a totally non-political sense. So the word 'command' or hukm in this sentence can never be taken to refer to political power.

To support the claims of political Islam, yet another argument is put forward, that, when God decided to create Adam, He said to the angels:

'I am going to place a khalifah on the earth.' (2:30)

Referring to this verse, they maintain that khalifah means vicegerent. In other words, God has created man so that he may establish a system of justice on earth as God's vicegerent.

Furthermore, they point out that God imposed His 'command' or hukm on the material world, but not on the human world. In the human world, God wants man to enforce divine commands on His behalf. This divine vicegerency or khilaafah will be conferred on those who have complete faith in God.

This interpretation is totally illogical. In Arabic, khalifah means 'successor', not 'vicegerent' for which the word *naib* is used. So it is inconceivable that man should become God's successor.

Man may be a successor to some creature of God but never the successor to the Creator Himself. Before creating man, God had given earth into the possession of other creatures. These predecessors of man had caused bloodshed on earth, so God removed them and settled man in their place.[1]

We learn, moreover, from other verses of the Quran, that man has been sent to the world in order to be tested.

'He created death; He created life to test you.' (67:2)

That is, only after this test will it be clear who is worthy of Paradise and who is to be consigned to hellfire. It is obvious that while a successor to a creature can be put to the test, the test of a vicegerent of God is inconceivable. This means that this projection of man as one who will enforce God's commands must be rejected outright.

So it is entirely unscientific to build up the theory of political Islam out of this verse:

'I am creating a successor on earth.' (2:30)

Also, if the verse had actually meant man to be the successor to God, it would amount to admitting that God's plan had never been fulfilled, even though He had sent 1,24,000 prophets to earth; it would mean that no prophet had succeeded in establishing God's desired system on earth in the capacity of being His vicegerent. Even the first man and a prophet, Adam, failed to establish this system. In his own lifetime, one of his sons killed his own brother (5:30).

Another verse of the Quran which is quoted as the basis of this political theory of Islam reads:

'It is He who has sent His Messenger with guidance and the religion of Truth, so that He may make it prevail [ideologically] over every other religion, however much the polytheists may hate this.' (9:33)

On a closer inspection of the wording of this verse, we find that what has been said here has nothing to do with politics. It describes a situation which is religious in nature, that is, the ascendancy of monotheism over polytheism.

The word 'superiority' or *izhaar* occurs here in this verse. Izhaar does not imply extirpation or abolishment. It means proving superiority, or ascendancy, through arguments. In the time of the Prophet of Islam, polytheism dominated Arabia. The entire popular culture was polytheistic. But, as we know, there was no polytheistic rule at that time in Arabia in the political sense—no ruler was considered divine and worshipped. What existed was belief in polytheism or idol worship, in support of which people had devised certain arguments of their own. The mission of the Prophet was to refute these arguments and prove the superiority of monotheistic religion by means of counter-arguments.

Another of the arguments given in support of the political theory of Islam relates to the following verse:

'Fight them until there is no more [religious] persecution and religion belongs wholly to God.' (8:39)

What is called persecution (*fitna*) in this verse refers to a state of affairs which was brought to an end during the lifetime of the Prophet and his companions. According to this verse, what was aimed at was not a simple matter of fighting (qital), but putting a stop to the persecution of the believers and ensuring the freedom to worship the one and only God. This being so, we shall have to determine what exactly has been called fitna in the Quran and furthermore how, during the early phase itself, it came to an end.

According to Abdullah ibn Umar, a senior companion of the Prophet, fitna here means religious persecution.[2] In earlier times, all over the world, including Arabia, religious persecution was prevalent in all walks of life. Except for the state religion, no other religion was tolerated. Religious tolerance and religious freedom were unknown. In view of this situation, the Prophet and his companions were commanded to put an end to this system of persecution with all the power at their disposal—they were to usher in an age of religious freedom throughout the world.

But, as the period when Prophet Muhammad began to spread the message of monotheism in Arabia was rampant with religious persecution, people put up stiff resistance to his call, though his methods were entirely peaceful. When their opposition failed to root out his movement, they took to violence to stop his efforts. The Prophet, choosing to avoid conflict, migrated from Makkah to Madinah. At a later stage, his opponents took the path of armed aggression; as a result, the Prophet had to wage four defensive battles which were more like skirmishes, each lasting only for half a day. Nonetheless, his movement went on spreading and his opponents ultimately suffered total defeat. Subsequently, the whole of Arabia abandoned all opposition and accepted monotheism.

Thus, in the Prophet's own lifetime, religious persecution was brought to an end in Arabia. However, the two great empires of that period, the Sassanid and the Byzantine, which, directly or indirectly, ruled over large parts of Asia and Africa, were not ready to accept any religion other than that of the state, and so continued to practise religious persecution.

When the Arabs accepted Islam, both these empires found the situation intolerable. They considered it very dangerous that any religion other than their own should spread in contiguous territories. To obliterate the new religion, they initiated hostilities against the Arabs who had embraced Islam. Prophet Muhammad and his companions were thus compelled to wage several defensive wars against these empires. Both the empires—the Sassanid and the Byzantine—were dismembered within a very short span of time. With that, within and outside Arabia, religious persecution was rooted out. A new historical phase which was based on the principle of religious freedom rather than on religious coercion set in. In this way, a new liberating process that culminated in Europe in the French Revolution was initiated.

The Prophet and his companions were thus instrumental in overthrowing political powers based on religious coercion. Europe put an end to religious coercion at a much later stage. Ultimately, the historical process, initiated in the seventh century and given such a strong impetus by Prophet Muhammad, culminated in the twentieth century in total religious and intellectual freedom. Today, all over the world, religious freedom has come to be accepted as an absolute human right. The crystallization of this historical process was enshrined in the Charter of the United Nations, to which all the nations of the world became signatories after the Second World War. It was thus finally accepted that religious freedom was man's absolute right—on no pretext could this right be withheld from him.

To repeat, the above-mentioned verse about fighting persecution has nothing to do with the notion of political

Islam. It only means that political coercion be brought to an end so that all individuals, both men and women, may lead their lives in an atmosphere of religious freedom. Man should have full freedom to adopt a religion of his own choice, without any coercion or pressure.

According to Islamic belief, God designed this world as a testing ground. Every man or woman born into this world is undergoing a trial. God has given everyone freedom so that he may be tested. That is why any system devised to abolish human freedom goes against the very Creation Plan of God. He has certainly not granted this freedom in order to jeopardize His own Creation Plan.

That is why, whenever any system aimed at abolishing human freedom emerges, God destroys that system. The kingdoms of old and their religious systems were established on the principle of coercion—that is why God did not allow them to flourish. The communist system, established in the Soviet Union, also ruled out the possibility of religious freedom and was likewise destroyed by God so that religious freedom might be restored.

The command that the Prophet and his companions were given to wipe out this religious persecution (fitna) was also of the same nature. Its goal was essentially to put an end to religious coercion and to usher in a new age of religious freedom. This command has nothing to do with political Islam, nor does it have anything to do with the theory put forward by present-day extremist Muslims that they are duty-bound to fight to establish Islamic rule all over the world.

13

Negative Thinking Alien to Islam

When any community—be it religious, ethnic or linguistic—thinks negatively about any other community, it is often because it imagines that community to be responsible for all its suffering. But there is no room whatsoever for negative thinking of any kind in Islam. God has unequivocally stated:

'Whatever misfortune befalls you is of your own doing.' (42:30)

According to Islamic teaching, whenever any misfortune befalls us, we should not blame others but, by a process of introspection, should pinpoint our own shortcomings—the real cause of misfortune—and then attempt to rectify them. What one definitely must not do is nurture feelings of hatred and revenge for those one holds responsible for one's misfortunes; this is in no way lawful in Islam and only increases one's own suffering.

This truth is expressed in different ways in the Hadith and the Quran. The Quran states:

'And do not become faint of heart nor grieve—you
will have the upper hand if you are believers.'
(3:139)

Furthermore, we learn from the Quran that the enemy
is actually the product of our own shortcomings. Otherwise,
the enemy has no concrete external existence. There is a
verse in the Quran to this effect:

'If you persevere and fear God, their designs will
never harm you in the least.' (3:120)

From this we learn that the actual problem for believers
is not the hatching of plots against them by their enemies,
but their own lack of patience and their own failure to remain
God-fearing. If the believers were patient and God-fearing,
their enemies would be incapable of doing them any harm.

A practical example of this principle is clearly
demonstrated in the Quranic account of the Battle of Uhud,
in which Muslims suffered great losses. This battle took place
in the third year after the Prophet had migrated to Madinah.
That it was a clear case of aggression on the part of the
Prophet's opponents is obvious as the fighting took place
on the outskirts of Madinah; the opponents had travelled
about 300 miles from Makkah to launch their attack. But
when the Quran commented upon this battle, it did not
refer to the injustice and plots of the aggressors, but rather
held the Muslims responsible, saying that they had to suffer
such a great loss owing to their internal shortcomings:

'But then your courage failed you and you disagreed among yourselves.' (3:152)

The next verse, 153 of the third chapter of the Quran, clearly tells Muslims not to hold others responsible for their defeat and losses in the Battle of Uhud. Instead of blaming others, they are exhorted to reform themselves.

For further clarification of this issue, we shall have to take into account another divine law, which is of particular relevance to the People of the Book. Before the advent of Prophet Muhammad, this law applied to the Jews, the former People of the Book. Now it is applicable to the Muslim community or ummah who, after the advent of Prophet Muhammad, hold the position of the People of the Book.

With reference to this divine law, the Quran says of the Jews:

'We forewarned the Children of Israel in the Scripture, "Twice you shall commit evil in the land. You shall become great transgressors." When the time of the first of these warnings came, We sent against you servants of Ours, of great might, who ravaged your homes. So the warning was fulfilled, and after a time We allowed you to prevail over them once again and aided you with wealth and offspring and made you great in number. [We said], "If you persevere in doing good, you will be doing good to yourselves; but if you do evil, it will go against you." When the time of the second warning came, [We roused against you others] to disgrace you utterly and to enter the place of worship as they had entered it before, utterly destroying all that they laid their hands on. We said, "Your Lord may yet have mercy on you, but if you do the same again, so shall We: We have made Hell a prison for those who deny the truth."' (17:4–8)

This verse mentions two incidents from Jewish history when non-Jewish rulers, Nebuchadnezzar of Babylonia (Iraq) and the Roman emperor Titus, attacked the Jews in 586 BC and AD 70 respectively, causing great havoc. But the Quran does not classify these violent episodes as cases of injustice and tyranny (zulm), committed by oppressor kings against the Jews. On the contrary, God attributed these events to Himself, saying that the attackers were God's servants who had been sent to Palestine to implement a divine plan.

We learn from the Quran and the Hadith that, being People of the Book, the Muslims are in no different a position from that of the Jews. When perversion sets in among Muslims, God may send down punishments to them by way of warning, through some of His servants. At such times, Muslims, instead of viewing this as oppression wrought by an oppressor, should take it as a warning sent by God. On all such occasions, Muslims, instead of holding someone to be their enemy and then launching campaigns of hatred and violence against him, should rather take to introspection and devote themselves to self-reform.

For a period of about one thousand years after the emergence of Islam, Muslims believed in personal introspection. Before the age of the printing press and the media, there was little reading material for Muslims beyond the Quran and the Hadith, whose teachings moulded their thinking. In situations of adversity, instead of holding others guilty, hating them and seeking to extract revenge, Muslims were given to introspection. This is illustrated by the following historical examples.

In the thirteenth century, the militant Tartar tribes inhabiting the hilly regions of Turkestan invaded the Muslim empire, destroying the entire area from Samarqand to Haleb. There were scenes of fire and bloodshed everywhere. Apparently, it was a case of aggression by outsiders. But the religious scholars of those times did not succumb to the kind of negativism indulged in by present-day Muslim leaders in all such matters.

The famous Muslim historian Izzuddin ibn al-Asir (d. 1232), a witness to the entire Tartar onslaught, wrote a book, *Al-Kamil fi at Tarikh*, based on his own personal experience and observations in which he gave details of the tragic events. He begins his description of the calamity with these words:

> For many years, I shrank from giving an account of these most horrible events. Even now I am reluctant to the task, for who would find it easy to sing the death-song of Islam and Muslims. Would that my mother had not given birth to me, would that I had become non-existent. If anyone says that no similar

tragedy has ever befallen humanity, right from the
time of Adam to this very day, he would certainly
be right.[1]

However, ibn al-Asir, unlike present-day Muslims, did
not talk of hatred for and revenge upon the attackers, or
curse them and hold them to be criminals. On the contrary,
he held the Muslims themselves responsible for this tragedy.
He wrote that the Muslim ruler of Iran, Khwarazm Shah,
had the Tartar traders killed and their goods looted. When
this news reached Genghis Khan, the Tartar chief, he was
enraged and vowed to destroy the Muslim empire. He began
a trail of destruction from Samarqand that went on until
his grandson Hulagu completed it.

Let us take another example. Nadir Shah, the king of
Iran, notorious for his tyranny and harshness, attacked India
in 1739 and advanced on Delhi. After conquering Delhi, he
gave orders for a general massacre of the inhabitants. His
actual purpose was to loot gold and silver. He then went
back, taking with him the peacock throne, the Kohinoor
diamond and many other valuable objects.

Even after this appalling tragedy, the Muslim scholars
of the time did not react as present-day Muslims would.
Rather they felt that, in this instance, what was needed
was introspection. A famous religious scholar of the time,
Mirza Mazhar Jan-i-Janan (d. 1781), commented thus on
the tragic aftermath of Nadir Shah's invasion: '*Shaamat-
e-Aamal-e-ma Surat-e-Nadir girift.*'[2] (What Nadir Shah
perpetrated was not Nadir Shah's tyranny. It was rather
our [evil] actions, which took the form of Nadir Shah.)

A negative reaction to all such incidents by Muslim writers and speakers is a purely present-day phenomenon. Pick up any Muslim magazine or newspaper today and you will find that any incident which goes against Muslim interests will be projected as oppression and the result of a plot by other nations. This kind of negative reporting is so common that perhaps it is without exception. It is this negative reporting by the Muslim media which gives the greatest stimulus to the violent thinking of today's terrorists.

In my experience, this manner of negative reporting started largely with the coming of age in modern times of the print media. In modern journalism, there is a particular method of news reporting called the inverted pyramid, that is, starting the report not at the beginning of an incident but at the point of its culmination.

For instance, suppose there is a dispute between two people over money in New Delhi, and it causes such enmity to flare up between them that one of them is bent on killing the other. He pursues his 'enemy' until one day he finds him sitting all alone in a park, and he kills him. When this crime is reported in the newspaper, the actual order of the events will not be adhered to, with the reader being told about the murder at the end. Rather, the very first sentence of the news would be: 'Murder in a New Delhi Park'.

This method of reporting is against nature. The Quran, which is the book of nature, gives us, in chapter 12, an example of correct reporting. In this chapter titled 'Joseph', the reader is informed about important incidents in the life of Prophet Joseph in the chronological order. This style of reporting shapes the reader's mind in a natural way, while in journalistic reporting the reader's mind is shaped in an unnatural way. The picture registered in his mind is thus out of line with historical facts.

The major failing of this method of reporting is that it generally highlights the latter half of the story and either leaves out the first half altogether or narrates it inaccurately. Muslims, too, follow this form, consciously or unconsciously. This method has become so popular that, in the age of the press, all Muslim writers and speakers have begun to write and speak in this same manner. This unnatural method is condemned in Islam. In the eighty-third chapter of the Quran, it is called 'at tatfif' (short-measure):

> 'Woe to those who give short measure; those who, when they take a measure from people, exact full measure, but when they give them a measure or weight, hand over less than is due.' (83: 1–3)

Due to this style of reporting, the Muslim media have been so filled with negative news that readers cannot but think negatively. And it is this negativity that has culminated in the horrendous violence of terrorism.

Today's violent jihad has risen principally from a feeling of negativity in Muslim minds, instilled by a falsifying media and fuelled by an incompetent leadership. Trying to compensate for an earlier loss—whether real or imagined—by resorting to feelings of hatred and a desire for vengeance only compounds one's miseries. Each such step is against the law of nature. And no such action will ever succeed in this world of God.

14

Jihad or Terrorism

Anyone making a study of Muslim terrorism has no option but to deal with the word 'jihad'. It is taken for granted that 'Islamic terrorism' means terrorism in the name of Islam. A *mujahid* is thus defined as one who actively devotes himself to the obliteration of his enemies. But in the words of the Quran (2:205), such actions as this should not be defined as jihad, but as *fasad* or corruption.

In its literal sense, 'jihad' in Arabic simply means struggle—striving to one's utmost to further a worthy cause.

For instance, in the Quran (25:52), the peaceful communication of the Islamic message of monotheism is referred to as 'jihad'. The word 'jihad' has even been used in a Hadith to mean taking proper care of parents. Moreover, Prophet Muhammad once observed:

'A mujahid is one who struggles (performs jihad) with his own self, so that he may surrender to God.'[1]

War is allowed in Islam only for one purpose and that is defence (9:13). In the Quran, the word used for defensive war is qital (22:39).

However, in its extended sense, qital can also be called jihad. But as Islam sets certain conditions for the proper performance of all actions, similarly, there are necessary conditions for defensive war. For instance, it is an established principle in Islam that war can be waged only by a properly established government.[2] Individuals and non-governmental organizations are definitely not permitted to wage an armed struggle. To them, Islam allows only peaceful struggle.

Muslim individuals or organizations are not allowed under any circumstances to initiate an armed struggle, even on the grounds of suffering oppression or aggression. Engaging in hostilities through guerrilla or proxy warfare is necessarily unlawful in Islam. While defensive war on the part of the state is lawful, war waged by non-governmental organizations clearly falls into the category of terrorism.

Some people have extended the word 'terrorism' to include the notion of 'state terrorism'. In their view, the US attack on Iraq in 2003 is an instance of state terrorism. This is a grave fallacy. For, while the use of weapons by non-governmental organizations is unlawful, it is certainly lawful for an established government to do so. It is totally unlawful for a non-governmental organization to be involved in an act of war. But if one state attacks another and does it for other than defensive purposes, no matter what the pretext, it may at most be regarded as having misused its powers. Indulging in such an action, which is unwarranted, is an offence, but rather than calling it 'state terrorism' it should instead be classified as a case of misuse of authority.

Thus if one country attacks another, and the government is forced to take defensive measures against the aggressor, its course of action will remain entirely within the ambit of the principles laid down by the United Nations. The state has the right to use arms, provided it does not violate international norms. But non-governmental organizations have no such right at all. If a non-governmental organization uses arms, its case would be an unauthorized use of arms. While if a state uses arms violating international norms, its case is one of misuse of arms.

So, when any individual who is at the head of a clandestine organization and not of a properly established government wages war, he is clearly a terrorist rather than a mujahid. His activities are examples of corruption or fasad, and are in no way examples of true jihadi activities.

In his best-selling book *The Clash of Civilizations and the Remaking of World Order*, Samuel Huntington sets out to show that, in the case of the earlier Crusades, the West was defeated by Islam, and that in the world of today there is another ongoing crusade. Once again, according to the author, the West is face to face with Islam. He observes: 'After the fall of communism, Islam is the new enemy to the West.'

There are many people today who endorse such views. Individuals like bin Laden, who are in the process of waging an armed struggle against the West, are viewed in this light. That is why we often come across the view that a second crusade is being fought between the Muslim world and the Christian world.

But this proposition is wholly baseless. The present confrontation has nothing to do with Islam or jihad, and is in no way a war such as the Crusades were. The Crusades took place between Muslim and Christian rulers, whereas the present armed confrontation is between Muslim guerrillas and the West at large.

So far as the medieval Crusades were concerned, their object was the recovery of Palestine, and to this end the Christian rulers of Europe launched an extended military operation. A war was then waged by the Muslim state in the defence of the land. And the war continued intermittently for about 200 years. But in that instance, the war was quite justifiable, because it was the Muslim state that was at the helm of military affairs throughout the period. The case today is diametrically different. The sporadic outbursts of violent activities at different places in the name of jihad are not being engaged in, or even overseen, by any Muslim government, but are the work of a number of non-governmental individuals and organizations who, as already shown above, have no right to engage in an armed conflict.

During the lifetime of the Prophet, an individual called Musailema, from Yemen, rebelled and claimed that he himself was a prophet. (This incident has been recorded in different historical texts.) He sent a two-member delegation to the Prophet with this message: 'I am a co-partner in prophethood. So you should believe in my prophethood and half the territory of Arabia will be yours and half will be mine.'[3]

Prophet Muhammad questioned the messengers about their views on Musailema. They replied that they shared

Musailema's beliefs. On hearing this, the Prophet of Islam said: 'Were messengers not to be killed, I would have you killed.'[4] This shows that Islamic law in international affairs is the same as has been accepted by other nations; international norms are also the norms of Islam. Only those things which have been explicitly declared unlawful are exempted from this adherence to international norms.

Seen in this light, jihad (in the sense of war or qital) can be rightly defined as such military activities as are internationally accepted, while terrorism covers such military activities as are internationally held to be illegal. Islam advocates enforcing its own laws in internal matters, but so far as international affairs are concerned, the same principles as are accepted by other nations will be followed by Islam.

In modern times, most governments have a constitution. Similarly, the majority of the nations subscribe to an overarching body, the United Nations, which has its own charter. Today, every country enjoys the right to deal with its internal matters according to its own constitution. But in international affairs, it has been unanimously accepted by all member-nations of the United Nations that they will be bound by the decisions of that organization.

This applies also to Islam, which follows these same principles. In both internal and external matters, the followers of Islam will honour exactly the same precepts as those honoured by other nations. The truth is that Islam is a religion of adjustment rather than of confrontation.

15

Arguments against Suicide Bombing

Religion-based terrorism is perhaps the most dangerous phenomenon of Muslim history. Throughout Islamic history, until very recently, action has always meant result-oriented action. But in modern times, for the first time, the Muslim mindset has become so distorted that, on occasion, fruitless action has also come to be considered desirable. Suicide bombing, which shows a preference for death over life, falls into this category.

How has the act of suicide come to be rated so highly as a solution to political problems? It is not traceable to some special devotional attachment to Islam, but is due rather to an inimical attitude towards man. As the suicide bomber ties the bombs on to his body, it is not pro-Islamic, but rather anti-humanity sentiments which motivate him to adopt such a deadly course. No one in his senses can deny this.

In the twentieth century, Muslims set about to take back the lands which had been usurped by their enemies, with the Palestinian issue being the focal point around which this violent thinking was developed. In 1948, Hassan al Banna lived up to the spirit of the times and took out an anti-Israel procession with the slogan 'Labbaik ya Falastin, Labbaik ya Falastin' (We are here to answer your call, O Palestine, we are here to answer your call, O Palestine). Yet, despite a very long struggle, the plan did not meet with success. Quite the reverse ensued. The greater part of Palestinc possessed by Muslims in 1948 has been taken away from them and they have been compelled to lead a life of much greater deprivation than before. Despite a sixty-year struggle, they gained nothing; instead they lost what was theirs to begin with.

According to the Quran, prophets are models for Muslims. And all the prophets, as we learn from the Quran, were well-wishers of mankind (7:93). But the common perception about the Islamists today is that they do not in their hearts possess any feelings of benevolence towards others. That they hold all non-Muslim nations to be their foes. That this animosity has reached levels where they are ready to cross all moral boundaries when it comes to attacking their supposed enemies. That if they think they can harm these foes by killing themselves, they are willing to take that extreme step too, by way of suicide bombing.

Extremist Muslim youths do indulge in such destructive thinking, but more distressing is the fact that Muslim scholars too think like this. Although Muslim religious scholars do not participate in such activities, they are fully engaged in providing ideological justification for this deadly campaign. They thus inspire and applaud the youths who opt for this suicidal course.

It is very strange indeed that Muslim religious scholars, particularly some Arab religious scholars, should look upon suicide bombing as an act to be appreciated and applauded. One example of such misplaced adulation appears in an article written by an Arab scholar, Dr Yousuf Al-Qarzawi, in which, instead of calling the act of suicide bombing 'suicide', he describes it as 'the desire to seek martyrdom'.[1] Muslim religious scholars have made every effort to justify this act of suicide by 'proving' it to be lawful. But the arguments they have put forward are entirely baseless. An analysis of some of their arguments is presented here.

One supposedly relevant verse of the Quran is quoted in support of the argument that the act of suicide can be equated with 'frightening off enemies'. The Quranic verse from which this argument is derived reads as follows:

'Prepare any strength you can muster against them, and any cavalry with which you can overawe God's enemy and your own enemy.' (8:60)

This verse speaks of striking 'terror into the enemy of God'. But this has nothing to do with committing suicide. What the verse specifically underlines is the significance of the preparations to be made. That is, Muslims should make themselves sufficiently strong so that their enemies will remain in awe of them and will be discouraged from being aggressive.

In other words, this verse offers us a peaceful strategy to counter the enemy, rather than killing oneself in the name of inflicting harm upon him.

Another argument in favour of suicide bombing is 'supported' by references to the wars which took place in the early days of Islam. However, this argument ignores the fact that such wars were waged to fend off some aggressor or the other and were purely defensive in nature.

As a general rule, there are occasions in war when combatants, in this case Muslims, have to take risks to attack the enemy. But only by misinterpretation can such incidents be cited to provide justification for suicide bombing.

One such incident took place in the days of the first caliph, Abu Bakr, when Musaylama ibn Thamama, a leader of Yemen, revolted. (Yemen had come within the fold of the Islamic state during Prophet Muhammad's lifetime.) To suppress this revolt, the first caliph sent out an army. In the final stage of this war, Musaylama's army was forced to retreat, but while fleeing, it gained entry into an orchard in Yamama, which had a high stone-wall boundary and a strong gate.

This was not the age of helicopters. So it seemed well-nigh impossible for the caliph's army to pursue the rebels into the orchard. As we learn from historical records, at that juncture, Bara'a ibn Malik, one of the caliph's soldiers, used a stratagem to overcome the difficulty. He told his fellow soldiers that he would sit on a shield which they should hold up with arrows, so that he could scale the wall. They did as he suggested, and he was able to reach the top of the wall from where he jumped inside. He was immediately attacked by Musaylama's men, but somehow he managed to open the gate. The Muslim army rapidly poured through the gate, fought Musaylama's army, finally routing it. Musaylama himself was killed.[2]

Referring to this incident, the supporters of suicide bombing hold that the step taken by Bara'a ibn Malik was on the same lines as suicide bombing, and that this example set by a companion of the Prophet provides the justification for suicide bombing. But this argument is false and quite baseless.

Suicide bombing is a strategy—made possible by the invention of explosives—whereby an individual kills himself or herself with the sole aim of harming the enemy. The incident relating to Bara'a ibn Malik is in no way an example of a suicidal step, but an example of a brave man taking risks to make an effective attack on the enemy. He may be risking his life, but he is not out to kill himself. Indeed, soldiers do have to take such risks in wartime.

The suicide bomber, however, decides in advance that he must die. When the bomb tied to his body explodes, he will surely be blown to shreds. There is no chance of his survival. But the incident involving Bara'a ibn Malik is of a totally different kind. He certainly took a step that entailed great risk, but he did not try to kill himself on purpose. Ultimately, he was successful in his ploy, did not die and lived on for many more years.

The truth of the matter is that suicide is totally forbidden (haram) in Islam. Under no circumstances whatsoever is suicide lawful. It is forbidden to the point where, if someone is dying and it is certain that he will not survive, even in his final moments, Islam does not allow him to take his own life.

An incident illustrating this Islamic tenet has been recorded in Sahih Muslim (the second most authentic book of the collections of the Hadith). It took place during the lifetime of the Prophet at the Battle of Khaybar. Quzmanuz

Zufra, a soldier from the Muslim side, fought very bravely and met his death. The Muslims said that he was a martyr and would go to Paradise. But the Prophet said that he would go to hell. The companions were astonished.

So the Prophet asked them to find out the cause of his death. On inquiry, it was discovered that he had indeed fought very bravely for the Muslims and then had fallen down gravely wounded. But then, finding the pain of his injury unbearable, he ended his life with his sword.[3]

The Prophet's disapproval of his action makes it clear that in Islam life is so precious that it can never be terminated at will on any pretext. Islam is a harbinger of life and gives no licence for euthanasia. This is why the virtue of patience is given the utmost importance in Islam. Patience (sabr) means tolerating the severest affliction rather than taking any such step as putting an end to one's life.

The history of the present-day kind of jihad by Muslims can be traced to the colonial period, when the European nations, particularly Britain and France, took control, directly or indirectly, of the Muslim world. With this turn of events, Muslim movements were launched against Western colonialism in Asia and Africa. The Second World War greatly weakened the European nations. This went in favour of the Muslim freedom fighters, eventually bringing to an end the political domination of Muslim countries by Western colonial powers.

Later, the Soviet Union's army invaded Afghanistan and, with the help of the local communist party, succeeded in establishing USSR's political dominion. Given this untenable state of affairs, Muslim fighters took up arms against Russia.

Since the Soviet Union's expansion was harmful to American interests, the United States gave its full support to the Muslims fighting against Russia. With American support, the Muslim fighters or mujahidin emerged victorious and Russia was compelled to leave Afghanistan.

A similar event took place in 1967 in Palestine. The situation prevailing after the Six Day War gave Israel an opportunity to extend its territory by capturing the border areas of Syria, Egypt and Jordan. This enraged not only the Arabs, but Muslims all over the world; so, with the global support of Muslims, the Palestinians went on to wage an armed war against Israel. This war initially targeted only Israel, but when the mujahidin saw that America was giving its full support to Israel, hostilities were extended against America too. It was in the war against America that bin Laden emerged as a hero.

But, as we know, the war waged for the Palestinian cause met with total defeat, bringing nothing but destruction to the Muslims. The Muslims became so frustrated that they were willing to take such drastic steps as suicide bombing. But suicide bombing has no merit as a military strategy—it is merely a futile, destructive activity carried out as a result of a total sense of frustration.

Why did Muslims meet with such poor results on the Palestine front? The reasons can be traced to incompetent Muslim leaders. As mentioned above, the Muslims owed their success in overcoming colonialism to the after-effects of the Second World War. Similarly, the mujahidin met with success in Afghanistan only because of the total support given to them by the Americans. But the Muslim leaders unrealistically attributed both these successes exclusively to the military prowess of the mujahidin. The mujahidin were convinced that it was they alone, by their own sacrifices, who had earned those successes.

It was this false assumption that gave them a shot in the arm in their conflict against Israel. However, despite extraordinary sacrifices, they met with total defeat. The sole reason for this was that on the Israeli front the mujahidin had to fight on their own. In this case, they had no external power to come to their assistance. The difference in the fighting capacity between the mujahidin and Israel was too great for the mujahidin to have ever succeeded in their campaign.

The most unfortunate part was that no leader of any stature in the entire Muslim world emerged to impress upon the mujahidin the difference between the earlier battles and that against Israel, and to make it clear to them that Muslims would never receive any support on the Israeli front, not even from the United Nations. No one took it upon himself to urge them to refrain from armed confrontation and instead launch their movement in a peaceful sphere. It was this shortcoming on the part of the Muslim leaders which brought total failure to the mujahidin in Palestine.

16

Jihad against Muslim Rulers

As a matter of Islamic principle, the right to wage war or armed jihad is given only to an established Muslim state. No non-governmental individual, group or organization is allowed to take up arms, for such an initiative is absolutely unlawful, irrespective of the grounds offered for treading this path. This principle is set forth in *fiqh* (Islamic law) in this manner:

'To declare war is the prerogative of an established state.'[1]

According to Muslim leaders, Muslims today face problems that justify waging war against those they hold responsible. But Muslim rulers have not been willing to wage war.

Muslim leaders find this situation very frustrating. They maintain that these Muslim rulers have colluded with Western powers and have even been acting as their agents. In the light of this opinion, Muslim leaders now contend that such rulers are not true Muslims, but are, on the contrary, the enemies of Islam. Consequently, they engage in overt or covert militant campaigns (like guerrilla warfare) against these rulers. This battle continues to be waged in almost every Muslim country in one form or the other.

When we study this situation in the light of Islamic teachings, we find that a militant campaign against Muslim rulers is totally haram—it is in no way lawful. Under no circumstances are Muslims allowed to wage war against Muslim rulers. Even deviation from the right path by Muslim rulers provides no justification for such a war.

A number of traditions have been recorded in the books of the Hadith, under the chapter 'Kitab al-Fitan'. According to these traditions, the Prophet of Islam had predicted that after him a time would come when Muslim rulers would become degenerate, but that even then Muslims were not to engage in fighting to oust them. 'You had better break your sword, go to the jungles and graze goats, and in no circumstances fight against your rulers,'[2] observed the Prophet. Another Hadith says:

'Any one of you who finds in his ruler something which he dislikes ought to remain patient.'[3]

Yet another tradition of the Prophet guides us in this manner:

'Give the rulers the rights due to them and ask God for your rights.'[4]

This means that even if there is cause for complaint against the rulers, the subjects have to remain subservient to them and law-abiding. As regards the subject's dues, he should expect this from God alone. This is also exactly the teaching of Jesus Christ:

'Render therefore to Caesar the things that are Caesar's and to God the things that are God's.' (Luke 20:25)

Religious scholars are in agreement that the traditions of the Prophet clearly indicate that revolt against Muslim rulers is unlawful. Drawing on these traditions (recorded—as mentioned above—in the chapter 'Kitab al-Fitan'), Imam Nawavi, the commentator of *Sahih Muslim*, explains that in case anyone has any difference with or complaint against his rulers, he should convey his opinion to the rulers, quietly, in private meetings. He further writes:

'So far as revolt or armed confrontation (qital) is concerned, it is unlawful, and all Muslim scholars have agreed on this, even though the ruler is a sinner (*faasiq*) or an oppressor.'[5]

The injunction against Muslims waging war against Muslim rulers has great wisdom behind it. For, whenever such a war is waged, it will be between a regular army and the common people. Whereas a ruler can openly make preparations of all kinds, non-governmental organizations are constrained to carrying out limited and secret activities. Moreover, international law, while permitting rulers to engage in such activities, prohibits members of the public from pursuing similar actions.

For obvious reasons, whenever any non-governmental organization indulges in any act of rebellion, the ruler will exercise all his powers and take all possible measures to crush the revolt. This will result in Muslims fighting against Muslims, thus incurring huge loss of life and property. Under the guise of national security, the ruler will then put a ban on Islamic activities, thereby causing the loss of whatever opportunities that had formerly been available to Muslims to propagate their faith. The revolt against the ruler will thus prove counterproductive.

Most Muslim countries have gone through this after-effect of a revolt against Muslim rulers. In every Muslim country, under the guidance of zealous Muslim leaders, Muslims have launched militant movements against Muslim rulers, but the only result has been the further destruction of Muslims.

17

Who Are Kafirs?

One justification for violent jihad offered by those engaged in it is that all those targeted are kafirs and by killing them and purifying the earth of them the jihadis are carrying out a holy mission. This theory is wrong to the point of absurdity. Neither are the people so targeted kafirs, nor is there any other justification for killing them.

Basically, 'kafir' means a denier. The word kafir has never been used in the Quran to mean either an unbeliever or an infidel. In fact, this term was applied solely to the contemporaries of the Prophet—in particular, to people from the tribe of the Quraysh (chapter 109). The Prophet peacefully conveyed the divine message to them over a long period of time, but they refused to accept the truth of his words. The use of the word kafir for anyone other than the contemporaries of the Prophet is not permissible.

The most important thing to be grasped on this subject is that the word kafir denotes an individual rather than a certain race or community. It is in no way an appellation for a group. However, the generally held view is that those who are not Muslims are kafirs. This is an entirely baseless assumption. The word kafir is not synonymous with non-Muslim. According to Islam, the fact is that those who are not Muslims are simply human beings (insaan). We must look at them as such rather than classify them as kafirs. The right way, according to Islam, is to call each community or group by the name it has adopted for itself. For instance, America will be called America rather than the country of kafirs.

Prophet Muhammad received prophethood in AD 610. At that time, all the people, save him, were non-Muslims. When he addressed them to convey his message, he never said, 'O kafirs', but rather, 'O man' or 'O people'. He continued to use this form of address throughout his life. To him, all those who had not entered the fold of Islam were simply human beings.

There are a number of examples in the Quran of references to communities or groups of those times in which the names they themselves had adopted were used. Not once was the word kafir used. In the Makkan period, certain verses of the Quran were revealed which mention non-Muslims living outside Arabia. For instance, at the beginning of chapter 30, the Quran mentions the Byzantines who had temporarily been conquered by the Persians. The Byzantines at that time were Christians, but the verses do not say 'the Byzantine kafirs who have been defeated', but simply 'the Byzantines who have been defeated'. Similarly, chapter 105 of the Quran mentions Abraha, the non-Muslim ruler of Yemen, but it does not refer to him as a 'kafir ruler of Yemen', but rather as the 'man of the elephants'.

(Abraha's soldiers were mounted on elephants when he came to Makkah to attack the Kabah.)

It was only for the deniers of early Makkah that the Quran used the word 'kufr' and 'kafir', and that too after the Prophet had conveyed to them the message of Islam for as long as thirteen years. No one else, except the deniers of Makkah, was addressed in this manner.

The Quran says:

'Fight the leaders of disbelief.' (9:12)

This verse does not mean that you should start fighting whoever appears to you to be a kafir. Such a war has never been fought in Islam, nor is it lawful in Islam. It would be sheer madness to take this Quranic verse in any such general sense.

In this verse, the word kufr relates to certain events. That is, the cause of war is not the fact of others being kafirs, but rather their being aggressors. That is to say that those of the deniers who wage war with you must certainly be fought, but as a matter of defence (22:39). The actual meaning of the verse is clear from the following verse of the Quran:

'Will you not fight against those who have broken their oaths and conspired to banish the Messenger? They were the first to attack you. Do you fear them? Surely God is more deserving of your fear, if you are true believers.' (9:13)

At another place, the Quran has this to say:

'And fight in God's cause against those who wage war against you, but do not commit aggression— for surely, God does not love aggressors.' (2:190)

That is, do not be an aggressor, fight only in defence. There are a number of such verses in the Quran which show that war in Islam is not against denier per se, but against the aggressors. If someone is a denier, Muslims have been commanded to continue communicating the message of truth to him, peacefully and benevolently, rather than wage a war against him.

From the Islamic viewpoint, there is always a great risk involved in calling anyone a kafir, sinner or hypocrite, for hardly anyone but God can claim to know a person well enough to make such a pronouncement. That is why the Hadith gives us stern warning regarding such acts. Prophet Muhammad once observed:

'When someone calls a person kafir or faasiq (sinner) wrongly then such words will be returned to the caller.'[1]

That is to say, in the eyes of God, the caller himself will be held to be a kafir and faasiq. Anyone who is afraid of God's chastisement cannot call anyone kafir. It is only those whose hearts and minds are devoid of the fear of God who will do so. A true Muslim will fear calling anyone a kafir lest he himself be held a kafir in the eyes of God.

According to the teachings of the Quran, the right behaviour for man is to follow God's command. And so far as other people are concerned, he should never issue edicts against them. Rather, as their well-wisher, he should consider it his responsibility to convey God's message to them peacefully, till his last breath. All else relates to God, not man.

18

The Difference between Enemy and Attacker

Muslims who engage in violent activities in the name of jihad often cite atrocities committed against them as justification for their actions. They say that they are being oppressed and therefore a militant response is necessary to put an end to the oppression.

This is a grave misunderstanding. The truth is that Islam clearly differentiates between an enemy and an attacker. Indeed, there is no concept of offensive war in Islam—there is only defensive war. Only when an attack or aggression has taken place are there grounds for going to war in self-defence. A Muslim state certainly enjoys the right to take the necessary action to check aggression, once it is a proven case of aggression. But in the case of enmity, the situation is totally different. In Islam, enmity, whether open or hidden, does not justify the waging of an armed struggle against the enemy. Indeed, it is strictly prohibited. War may be waged only against an active aggressor, but not against a passive enemy.

Now the question arises as to what should be done when faced with the enemy in general. The Quran provides a clear guideline on this:

'Good and evil are not equal. Repel evil with what is better; then you will see that one who was once your enemy has become your dearest friend, but no one will be granted such goodness except those who exercise patience and self-restraint—no one is granted it save those who are truly fortunate.' (41:34–35)

The Quran clearly treats aggression and enmity as separate issues. Regarding aggression, the Quran has this to say:

'Permission to fight is granted to those who are attacked.' (22:39)

The teaching of Islam with reference to the enemy is totally different. As is clear from the verses quoted above, it advocates unilateral good behaviour towards the enemy. The benefit of such behaviour will be that today's enemy will become tomorrow's friend.

With this teaching, Islam has laid down the ground rules for international relations. As we learn from this verse, so long as a person is only an enemy and not an aggressor, attempts should be made by peaceful means to make him understand the error of his ways. Such measures as are taken must aim at softening his heart. In order to bring him closer, unilateral good behaviour should be demonstrated. This course of action should be adhered to until he either desists from his inimical actions, or else he resorts to aggression and thus compels Muslims to take defensive measures.

The same holds true in the attitude towards the oppressor, in that Islam does not advocate jihad against him. Islamic teachings exhort one to exercise patience or take the path of peaceful struggle. So far as armed jihad is concerned, it is forbidden (haram) against the oppressor, just as it is against the enemy. It is not lawful in Islam to fight against anyone except as a matter of sheer survival.

According to Islam, oppression is not a permanent phenomenon. Today's oppressor may tomorrow respond positively to peaceful persuasion, abandon his enmity and oppressive ways, and become just as we want him to be.

But oppression is also not just the result of purely evil intentions. More often than not, it is a desire for revenge on the part of the oppressed. It frequently happens that, having become enraged at the actions or attitude of some individual or group, one starts indulging in vengeful activities, which are termed as 'oppression' by the 'victims'.

This is why Islam forbids anyone being frivolously branded as an oppressor. The most effective strategy for checking oppression is to first take stock of one's own actions and discover the faults in oneself which, wittingly or unwittingly, have ignited the torch of revenge in the aggrieved party, thus turning him into an oppressor. However serious the situation, the first step, from an Islamic perspective, should be to discover the root cause of the problem and then to attempt to rectify matters.

19

Dealing with Oppression

If those who are engaged in violent jihad against their supposed enemies are questioned about their actions, they inevitably say, 'We are being oppressed, therefore we are fighting our oppressors.'

This answer seems 'technically correct', and also appears to carry weight from the moral standpoint. But it bears little relation to reality. To be realistic on the subject of oppression, one should examine it without bias. Moreover, this should be done in the light of the principle that any step against evil can be right only when it yields positive and beneficial results. If, in an effort to bring a lesser oppression to an end, one is faced with a far greater evil, then that step must be abandoned, for such a step would amount to committing suicide to save oneself from a small, temporary problem.

In this connection, one must remember that problems are a part of God's Creation Plan. They are not just the result of human action. The Creator has created this world as a testing ground. That is why He has given the freedom to everyone to make their own moral choices. Although oppression is a misuse of this freedom, the solution to this problem lies not in obliterating oppression per se, but rather in bringing it under some form of control which will act as a mitigating factor.

It can be likened to a thorn on a rose stem. If you are pricked by the thorn, you will not set about destroying the plant, but will instead try to find a way of dealing with it so that the chances of being hurt are reduced.

How should we define oppression? Oppression is the outcome of exploitation. For the exploiter, exploitation is the effort he makes to be successful in serving his own interests. But the one who is being exploited naturally sees it as oppression. Since, by the law of nature, exploitation can never be entirely rooted out, what the exploited need to do—instead of opting for the way of protest, complaint or violence—is adopt tactics which minimize or cancel out the effects of the exploitation. By utilizing their God-given intellect, they should convert the situation of exploitation into one of opportunity. Actually, the exploited have no other option.

As an illustration, let us take two examples which are in direct contrast to each other. One relates to the period of the British empire in India and the other to Japan after the Second World War.

As we know, the British ruled the Indian subcontinent until 15 August 1947. But much before they left, there was an upsurge in public feeling against British rule. As early as in 1834, the British government sent an English educationist, Lord Macaulay, from London to India to investigate the situation. After reviewing the circumstances, Lord Macaulay planned an educational scheme, on the basis of which the 'English system of education' was introduced into India. The objective of this measure, according to Macaulay, was to form a class of persons 'who may be interpreters between us and the millions whom we govern . . . Indian in blood and colour, but English in tastes, in opinions, in morals and in intellect'.

In accordance with this plan, the British government established institutions of English education all over the country. Now the Indian leaders had two options before them. One was to regard the British government's plan as a plot against the interests of the country and launch a campaign to foil it. The other option was to consider this plan of the British as an opportunity to make progress, and let the task of educating the country continue at its own pace.

But the Indian leaders of the time thought that by giving Indians an English education, the British government wanted to enslave India forever. To these leaders, taking no action in such a case amounted to giving their tacit assent to eternal bondage. Therefore, they launched a campaign against it.

The Indian leaders did all they could to foil the plan of English education. They instigated the students of schools and colleges to come out on to the streets and support their cause. The result was the eventual collapse of even the Indian educational traditions. The ensuing anarchy had to be remedied by the imposition of authoritarian discipline, and even today the sporadic turbulence observed in educational matters reflects the inadequacy of the measures taken at that time. Owing to this antagonistic campaign, the plan of giving Indians an English education met with only partial success. The anti-English feelings of the Indian leaders were so intense that, after gaining their freedom in 1947, they made every attempt to turn India into a Hindi-speaking nation.

Huge amounts of money were spent towards this end. However, the efforts proved fruitless. South India, which covers approximately half the area of the country, opposed this campaign. South Indians feared that if Hindi became prevalent, they would be deprived of government jobs. South India's opposition was so great that the leadership at the Centre felt there was a danger of the southern states breaking away and becoming a separate country like Pakistan.

Due to the pressure exerted by South India, the campaign to make India a Hindi-speaking country came to naught. If the British government's efforts to spread English education had continued unhampered, perhaps today India would have been one of the most powerful countries in the world. But owing to the unwise opposition to English, India lags far behind in progress and development. Today, it ranks as low as no. 128 on the Human Development Index.

Now let us take the example of Japan. In the Second World War, America defeated Japan and destroyed Hiroshima and Nagasaki, by dropping atomic bombs on them.

After the war, General McArthur was sent to Japan to oversee the reconstruction effort. The objective was the Americanization of Japan, so that the new Japanese generation could be permanently weaned away from military action against America and become America-friendly in its thinking.

In this case, too, a country was faced with two options. Japan could have either started a war of revenge against America or joined in the American reconstruction plan. But Japan's Emperor Hirohito surrendered and declared that, for the better future of Japan, the Japanese were ready to 'tolerate the intolerable'.

American officers devised a thirty-year plan for Japan, for the implementation of which the American government sanctioned a huge amount of money. The Americans on their part believed that after thirty years this would lead to the intellectual subjugation of Japan. Instead, Japan emerged as an economic superpower.

Before the Second World War, a similar situation confronted Muslim nations within the framework of the colonial system and the new world order of America. Western nations, equipped with modern resources, directly or indirectly dominated the Muslim world. This state of affairs demanded *ijtihaad*, that is, to strive to reapply the teachings of Islam in the changed scenario. But the Muslim leaders failed on this front, adopting instead the path of negative reaction. One who exercises ijtihaad succeeds in finding the path of positive response in any new or changed set of circumstances, but those who do not possess this virtue become victims of negativity and, when provoked, start fighting with their supposed adversary. This reaction results in nothing but destruction.

The entry of Western nations into the Eastern world was not like that of Genghis Khan or Nadir Shah. Western nations had also come equipped to initiate progress and development in the field of science and technology. Had the Muslim leaders possessed the ability to engage in ijtihaad, they would have learnt that this was a case of taking what is beneficial and leaving the rest. That is, they should have ignored the temporary political superiority of Western nations and, learning from the West's modern methods and accepting its help, set about educating their own people. Had the Muslim leaders done so, the period of adversity which came in the wake of Western colonization would have soon turned into one of glorious ease. But as a result of the negative response of the leaders, there could be no new and beneficial turn of events in Muslim world history.

The acts of terrorism perpetrated in the name of Islam are the product of the negative reaction of Muslim leaders to the modern age. Had the Muslim leadership been able to react in a timely and positive manner, these terrorists would have found themselves in a sphere where they could have actually played a positive role. Instead, they were led into playing the negative role of killing their supposed rivals and finally getting killed themselves.

After the Second World War, Japan adopted the path of positive response vis-à-vis America, with the result that today the scientific brains of Japan are engaged in producing top-quality goods and enriching Japan. On the other hand, the few Muslim scientists who exist are producing guns and bombs, so that they may annihilate their supposed enemies, not realizing that this will have a boomerang effect as can be seen in Pakistan.

20

Peace for the Sake of Peace

When terrorists are asked as to why they engage in activities which create anarchy, they reply, 'We too want peace. But true peace is one which is accompanied by justice. Peace without justice is no peace at all.'

This is the greatest fallacy entertained by the militants. When they, ostensibly seeking justice, stoop to violence, peace can never prevail. They ought to know, but seem not to, that in this world peace is simply a state in which the disturbances of warfare are absent. They should understand that the establishment of peace is desirable for the sake of peace. For it is peace that opens up opportunities for the kind of constructive activities which can seldom be accomplished in a situation where there is continual dislocation caused by clash and confrontation. Once people become tolerant and accept the reality and obtain peace for it own sake, what that actually does is open up opportunities. It creates favourable conditions which enable people to strive for their ideals, eventually attaining justice and other constructive ends. This happens due to the law of nature. When the individual refrains from making a controversial matter into one of prestige, this gives rise to serious thinking. This non-emotional thinking helps him to understand that if he were to walk out of the point of controversy he would find all other paths open to him. So it must be borne in mind that justice is not a direct result of peace. It is only by availing of the opportunities offered by peace that we can achieve justice.

So the maxim to follow when peace is desired in the state is: 'Ignore the problems, and avail of the opportunities.' This ideology of peace can counter the ideology of violence and it is based on the original sources of Islam.

The life of Prophet Muhammad provides a telling example of this wisdom. In the early period of Islam, when the Prophet was in Makkah, the city was under the domination of the Prophet's opponents. Meanwhile, the central place of worship in Makkah called the Kabah enjoyed the status of an international shrine. It was considered everyone's right to visit it without impediment.

In the sixth year of the Hijrah, when Prophet Muhammad had taken up residence in Madinah, he decided to go to Makkah and perform *umrah* (the minor pilgrimage). Accordingly, the Prophet set out for Makkah accompanied by 1500 companions. When the Prophet reached a place called Hudaybiyya situated on the outskirts of Makkah, he was stopped by Makkan leaders from entering the city. They insisted he go back to Madinah along with his companions. Since war on this occasion would otherwise have been inevitable, the Prophet initiated peaceful negotiations with the Makkans. These lasted for two weeks, at the end of which period a peace treaty was finally concluded. The gist of this treaty was that the Makkans had to agree to refrain from any military activity against Prophet Muhammad. The Hudaybiyya Treaty was thus the equivalent of a ten-year no-war pact. It took the form of a written pledge from the Prophet's opponents that they would not initiate any hostilities against him and that they would let him and his followers live in peace in Madinah.

The Hudaybiyya Treaty is, in fact, a peace treaty which was concluded not by receiving justice, but rather by leaving out justice from its ambit. All the conditions of this treaty were unilateral, giving concessions to the Makkan non-Muslims. None of these conditions were in favour of the Muslims. For instance, one article of the treaty was that the Prophet would not insist on going to Makkah to perform umrah, but would instead go back to Madinah directly from Hudaybiyya.

The treaty of Hudaybiyya was indeed a peace treaty, but the peace it ensured was not accompanied by justice, rather it was bereft of justice. Even so—as history tells us— it was this unilateral adjustment that led to the treaty which, in establishing peace between the two parties, gave the Muslims the opportunity to engage in activities which were more positive than just warding off enemy attacks. As a consequence, they were able to channellize all their time, energy and resources towards the consolidation of their nascent religion. The result was truly remarkable—within a short span of two years, Islam became so powerful that Makkah was brought into its fold without any fighting. That is why, referring to the treaty, the Quran stated:

'Truly, We have granted you a clear victory.' (48:1)

21

Democracy and Political Islam

The state of Muslim identity today is just the opposite of what Prophet Muhammad would have desired. He once observed:

> 'One who creates problems for his neighbours will not enter into Paradise.'[1]

And today, because of their erroneous notions, Muslims are perceived as a problem community everywhere.

The contemporary political version of Islam is one example of Muslims creating problems for others. Their interpretation of Islam has made their religion appear to be a complete political order, one which if not implemented as such, the believers cannot merit salvation. Therefore, they believe, they should even go to the extent of sacrificing their lives to establish Islam as a political institution.

When seen in the light of the sayings of Prophet Muhammad, this kind of political concept is nothing short of extremism. The Prophet maintained that any group which became extremist in religion would bring about its own destruction.[2] Many of today's Muslims fall into just such a category. On account of their extremist concept of religion, they have reached a point where they have become a problem not only for others but also for themselves.

The world of today has, by general consensus and as a matter of political principle, accepted the democratic system. The norm in democracy is 'Government of the people, by the people, for the people'. But this norm gets totally distorted in the political concept of Islamists. The Islamists' political formula seems to be 'Government of the Muslims, by the Muslims, for the Muslims'. This thinking has produced enormous problems for Muslims themselves.

The truth is that Islamists have produced a new version of Islam through a wrong interpretation of their religion. This new version comes into conflict with the world view of other groups. For instance, Islamists think that insulting Prophet Muhammad is such a great crime that the culprit should be killed forthwith. They believe that after committing this 'heinous crime' a human being has no right any more to live on this earth—the only thing befitting such a person is to purify the world of his existence. On the basis of this supposed principle, the Islamists declared that Salman Rushdie must be killed for the 'crime' he committed in writing a book in which he vilified the Prophet. They called for the same treatment to be meted out to the Danish publisher of some cartoons which showed extreme disrespect to the Prophet.

But today's world does not think on these lines. In fact, the thinking of today's world is quite the contrary. Freedom is a *summum bonum* in today's world. Everyone has freedom of thought and expression, in the absolute sense. It can be curtailed only when one inflicts physical injury in the exercise of this freedom, for instance, when one strikes or maims someone. So, it is but natural that Islamists have become unfit to live in such a world. They have become unwanted in a world which is alienating itself from them. These Muslims have become a problem community for the world from every point of view.

Moreover, many Muslims of today have formed a strange notion which they call the ummah: that Muslims all over the world are part of an international nation. According to this concept, the basis of nationhood of Muslims is their religion.

A universally acknowledged principle of the modern age is that the homeland is the basis of nationhood. The homeland of a man or a woman therefore determines his or her nationality. Accordingly, religion is a matter of private and personal belief, while nationhood is a secular matter and all issues pertaining to nationhood are decided according to secular principles. Thus, Muslims who cling to the notion that religion determines nationhood have become victims of a contradiction. Today, Muslims are living all over the world, but on account of their ideology, they are regarded with suspicion everywhere. It is generally believed that Muslims can be loyal only to a Muslim country, and that they cannot be loyal to a country where they are living as a religious minority.

22

The Role of the
Muslim Media

A terrorist is a product of hatred and this hatred is fostered by the media. This is the real cause behind the raising of certain individuals to the level of heroes. These so-called heroes and the media are so closely intertwined that the one cannot be understood without the other.

What is the mission of these self-proclaimed saviours of today's Islam? It is to take revenge upon the West on account of its oppression. According to them, oppression by the West existed in every age in one form or the other. For instance, they hold that it was the Western nations which put an end to the political empire of the Muslims. They ignore the fact that such changes of power are regular happenings in world history—as the dissolution of the Roman empire caused by the Sassanid empire, and the defeat of the Sassanid empire by the Roman empire. But in these two instances, there was no hatred in the conquered for the conqueror. It is also a fact that the Muslims, having established their rule by defeating the Jews and the Christians, too have done their share of conquering. Such events had repeatedly taken place in the past, but never before has such a jungle of hatred grown up as would produce the deadly phenomenon of modern-day terrorism in the name of Islam.

The reason for this unprecedented spreading of hatred is very simple. Incidents of this nature in the past took place before the age of the print and electronic media. In earlier times, the scene of both victory and defeat was the battlefield. Armies fought on the battlefield, lost or won the battle, and that was the end of the matter. The rest of the people who worked in their homes and fields were mostly ignorant of these events. That is why historiography was limited to recording events relating to kings and emperors and not to humanity in general.

But in modern times, when Western nations broke up the Muslim empire, the Jews occupied Palestine, America bombed Muslim Iraq or Muslim Afghanistan, the media reported every single incident and spread the news all over the world. In this way, all such incidents came to everyone's knowledge.

The role played by the media is of the utmost significance in that all the magazines and newspapers regularly give priority to publishing sensational speeches and writings by Muslims. The Muslim media of today are used for airing grievances and lodging protests. Muslim writers and speakers are now regularly engaged in telling the world through the media that the Western nations are oppressors and usurpers, and that the West feels nothing but enmity for the Muslim world and is plotting against it.

It is the Muslim media which has filled the minds of Muslims all over the world with feelings of hatred and revenge against non-Muslim nations. Muslim opinion of others has thus been marred by negativity. Had the modern media not existed, such instances of oppression would certainly have taken place as before, yet most Muslims would have continued to engage in their everyday activities, blissfully ignorant of all such happenings. The jungle of hatred would not have grown to yield so terrifying a harvest.

If you study the Quran, you will find that it is replete with positive teachings. According to the Quran, God is most Compassionate, most Merciful (1:2); Prophet Muhammad is a mercy to the world (21:107); the religion God sent through His messenger is the religion of mercy; and patience is the greatest form of worship (39:10).

Had the age of the media been ushered in a few hundred years ago, when Muslims were in power and they were not victims of oppression or usurpation, the media would have reported the positive teachings of Islam. Then the Muslims would have received the message that Islam wants them to deal with others compassionately and mercifully. But unfortunately, the modern media came into being only in the nineteenth and twentieth centuries when the Muslims were faced with what they termed oppression and exploitation. This problem of negativity is thus the product of an age when the Muslim media, contrary to the teachings of Islam, were filled with protests and complaints. The Muslim media had turned into an industry of negative propaganda.

In such circumstances, it was but natural that Muslims all over the world began to think negatively. Their hearts and minds were filled with feelings of animosity and lamentation, to the point where non-Muslim nations became objects of hatred to them, not of benevolence.

Furthermore, there is a feature common to both the Muslim and non-Muslim media, and that is selective reporting—by which positive news is left out and only negative news is projected, and that too in the most sensational manner. It is a fact that the media is an industry for the advertisement of negative news.

There have been many pieces of good news for Muslims in modern times. For instance, it was owing to their supposed 'enemies' that the printing press was invented, making it possible for the Quran to be printed in large numbers across the world, and thus be preserved and safeguarded for all eternity. It was again owing to these supposed 'enemies' that the wealth of petrol was unearthed, which proved to be the greatest source of prosperity for Muslims. It was these supposed 'oppressors' who brought into existence modern vehicles which greatly facilitated global travel. It was through these supposed 'oppressors' that universal communication was rendered possible, and the world thus became a global village. It was these same oppressors who invented methods of surgery which were painless. Western nations, held to be oppressors by Muslims, are the very nations which have brought into being the modern scientific age from which Muslims, like other communities, are reaping great benefits. But due to negative reporting by the Muslim media, many Muslims, consciously or unconsciously, have remained ignorant of the positive aspects of Western nations. They have been able to learn only of their negative aspects. The attitude of Muslims in modern times is expressed in this Arabic saying: 'People turn hostile to that of which they have no knowledge.'

Many Muslims may not have personally witnessed or experienced any case of oppression but, through the media, have learnt of all such events, both great and small, in terms highly exaggerated. Even more damaging is the fact that in the majority of the cases the media present only half of the story while heaping all the blame on the 'other' side.

In this way, the media have turned the minds of those tuned to their message into a jungle of prejudiced thinking, which is totally anti-Western in sentiment. Thus, with every terrorist incident becoming a matter of common knowledge right across the world, and any plot against the West, hatched by Muslim terrorists with the backing of an international support system of like-minded co-religionists, becoming world news, the media have indeed played a further role in escalating hatred and violence.

23

Intellectual Development in Religion

One principle of scientific study has been described in the Arabic words *tu'raful ashya' bi azdadiha*, that is, 'things are known by their opposites'. It is through comparison that we understand things the way they truly are.

Let us apply this principle to the study of a terrorist mind. Why are such destructive characters like terrorists born to religion and not to science? When we ponder this question, we arrive at a very important reality.

The truth is that there are two basic branches of knowledge. One, the science of matter, and the other, the science of the mind. All branches of knowledge stem from these two basic branches. The material, visible world is studied under the rubric of the science of matter, while the unseen world is studied under the rubric of the science of the mind. The science of matter is based on observation and experimentation. Any knowledge acquired through direct or indirect observation and experimentation becomes a part of the science of matter. It is diametrically opposite to the science of the mind where everything is based on speculation. That is why the branches of knowledge related to the science of matter are called exact sciences, whereas the branches of knowledge related to the science of the mind fall into the category of speculative sciences. There is a known and established way of settling differences in the sciences of matter. That is why such differences do not escalate into violence. However, when differences develop in the field of the sciences of the mind, it is not possible to reach a consensus. This is the reason differences escalate, leading to clash and confrontation.

For instance, a common man sees the sun and the moon in the sky. It appears to the naked eye that the sun and the moon are both equal in size. The observer then forms the opinion that the sun and the moon are equal in size, and that there is no difference between the two. However, modern astronomical instruments soon convince him that the sun is far bigger than the moon. In this way, any doubts or differences of opinion that anyone might have had about the size of the sun and the moon immediately come to an end. This is how differences are resolved in all the branches of the science of matter, paving the way for its disciplines to make commendable progress.

Let us take an example relating to the science of the mind. A certain person says that just as God is an omnipotent being with the power to work miracles, similarly, those pious individuals who have gone to their eternal rest too have comparable power. In this way, he accords a similar status to God and to those regarded as saints. Then another person claims that all power lies with God, no living or dead person is invested with any kind of power. Now the views of both differ and they start arguing to justify their respective stands. But their differences cannot be resolved because there exists no such clear-cut criterion like a telescope or a microscope which may decide the matter.

Thus, the sciences of matter produce unity of opinion while the sciences of the mind are reduced to a jungle of confusion.

Let us compare two examples to understand this issue. In olden times, astronomers had different views regarding the solar system. Some were of the opinion that the earth was at the centre of the solar system and the sun revolved around it, while others were convinced that it was the other way around—the first group supported the geocentric theory and the second the heliocentric one. Through observation and experimentation, a consensus was finally arrived at that the heliocentric theory was correct.

Now let us consider the other example. For thousands of years, man has been debating the question of what happens to him after death. Some are of the opinion that death is the very end of a man, while some others feel that there is life even after death. No unanimity has ever been achieved on this matter.

I have been struggling with this seeming lacuna in the sciences of the mind for many years. I wanted to know whether just as there was a clear criterion in the sciences of matter which is sufficient to settle differences, was there any criterion in the sciences of the mind which could settle differences similarly?

After a long study, finally I discovered the criterion. According to my experience and study, there is only one criterion and that is the Quran, the Book of God. It is due to this aspect of the Quran that it is called the standard or *muhaymin* (5:48).[1]

There are three major categories of the sciences of the mind—psychology, spirituality and religion. All three departments differ from the departments of the sciences of matter. There is no external criterion to give a concept an absolute form or a final shape. It is only the Book of God that enjoys the status of an absolute criterion. I would like to cite from the three fields of psychology, spirituality and religion to illustrate this point.

Let us first take the discipline of psychology. Psychology is the study of the human mind. However, so far, psychology has not been able to understand the human mind. The reason is that psychology does not have one definitive guide book. This fact has been explained by Alexis Carrel in his book *Man the Unknown* (1935).

Among the several schools of psychology, six are regarded as the major ones. But the dominant school of thought is the one attributed to the famous American psychologist John Broadus Watson (1878–1958). The theory devised by Watson is called behaviourism. Today, although behaviourism is not much in favour, it is still taught as a concept under classical psychology. The essence of behaviourism is that man is not made by nature, but by nurture. It holds that it is environmental events that form man and not his mind.

According to behaviourism, a person's mind or his thinking is influenced by the environment around him. It holds that the mind is not real, but relative; in other words, the mind is a product of the material environment.

This concept amounts to a total abrogation of the Islamic concept of life. According to Islam, the human mind is created for eternity. It has the capability to think and form opinions freely. The Islamic concept of accountability is related to the freedom of thought. But man's position becomes totally different in the behaviourist model—his position appears no different from that of animals. In the light of this theory, he does not enjoy any distinguishing position as compared to animals.

As regards man, this concept of behaviourism is based on a misunderstanding. That is, it regards a temporary phase to be a permanent phase. It is true that when a child is born it is influenced by its environment, until this environment becomes the greatest factor in shaping his personality. But this impression of the environment is superficial, not real. Animals also accept the influence of the environment. But in the case of animals this influence is an integral part of their personality, whereas in the case of man the influence of the environment on his personality is like onion layers. If these layers are removed, his original personality will be revealed just as it was at the time of his birth. Prophet Muhammad observed:

'Every child is born according to nature, it is his parents that make him either a Jew, or Zoroastrian or a Christian.'[2]

This means that man is born in his true nature, that is, divine nature. However, man is sent to be tested in a world where there are many different kinds of things. All these things influence his personality. This influence is called conditioning. This conditioning is at times too strong for man's actual personality to remain as it truly is. He deviates from his original nature he is born with.

However, man possesses willpower. His independent willpower is a part of his personality even after superficial conditioning. That is why it is always possible for man to de-condition his conditioned mind. He may remove the layers of conditioning from his mind and return to the original nature he was born with. The believers of behaviourism could not understand this reality. They regarded the conditioning by the environment as a permanent state and developed their ideology on that basis. Thus, the conditioned man came to be regarded as the real man.

The main reason for this approach was that it was based on the study of animals, for instance, mice, and the results of this study were applied to man. They saw that animals were influenced by their environment, and that their personality remained shaped by their environment till the very end. But there is a great mistake in this method of study. Animals have no willpower; therefore, they cannot de-condition themselves out of their own free will. Man, however, is totally a creature of willpower. At any time and in any environment, his willpower may be awakened and his conditioned mind can be changed.

In this respect, the human mind can be likened to an onion. In the centre of the onion, initially, there is a small kernel. Then layers start forming, one upon the other over this inner kernel. This process continues until the inner kernel is totally covered with external layers. Now, apparently, layers alone are visible. The kernel is completely covered and remains invisible. To find the kernel of the onion, all the external layers have to be removed. Similarly, all the conditioning has to be removed in order to restore man to his original pristine nature. This process of de-condiitoning is similar to the removal of onion layers.

The Quran states:

'Paradise is for those who purify themselves.' (20:76)

The word used here is *tazkia*, meaning purification. This refers to the removal of the superficial conditioning to reveal man's true nature.

The behaviourist school of psychology explored the process of man's conditioning, but not the process of his de-conditioning. It studied that aspect of his being which is similar to animals. But it did not study that part of man's being which is superior to animals, and the discovery of which can make him deserving of entry into Paradise.

Let us now take the case of spirituality. Spirituality has existed in the world in one form or the other for around five thousand years. But studies tell us that, despite such a long period, spirituality has not been able to make any noteworthy progress. It may not be wrong to say that the science of spirituality is still at the same point where it was around five thousand years ago, whereas material science has made tremendous progress within a very short period of time.

According to my experience, spirituality has failed to reach the starting point which is its actual source. History tells us that all the people who strive in the field of spirituality agree on the point that the source of spirituality lies within man himself. Therefore, man ought to practise meditation so that he may reach the source of spirituality and may acquire a spiritual personality.

This theory led to the development of self-centred spirituality. People wanted to gain entry into their inner self through long and hard spiritual exercises. The aid of song and dance was sought to achieve this end. But despite all efforts, what was finally achieved was nothing more than ecstasy. This is why spirituality, for all practical purposes, became a means of easing tension. In today's world, people usually live in tension and stress. Such people visit hospices of Sufis, ashrams or other spiritual centres so that they may ease their tension by practising different techniques of meditation. These techniques are based on the principle of stopping the thought process. One can say that the spiritual centres aim at temporarily stopping the process of thinking in the human mind, for tension is related to thinking. When man stops thinking, his tension will automatically come to an end. This act is called de-stressing.

If you ponder this fact deeply, you will realize that this process is not really de-stressing. It is instead de-humanizing. It brings man to the level of animals. This kind of action is a kind of anaesthesia, and nothing more. It is a fact that man is bestowed with the capacity to think and this is what distinguishes him from other creatures. True spirituality is that which leads man to intellectual development. Spirituality that stops the functioning of the mind spells intellectual death and can hardly be called spirituality.

According to the Quran, spirituality is based on *tawassum* (15:75), that is, taking lessons from God's signs. Here, realization can be attained by perusing creation. In this respect, the spirituality of the Quran may be called scientific spirituality.

Let us now take the matter of religion. The history of religion is as old as the history of man. But religion, too, met the same fate and was reduced to a stagnant discipline like the other two disciplines of the sciences of the mind— psychology and spirituality. Religion could not match the tremendous progress made by material science. This was because, after some generations, religion was replaced with its reduced form. Etiquette and rituals came to be regarded as religion; intellectual exercise was replaced with a set of rituals.

All religions regard rituals as synonymous with religion today. That is why people fail to receive any benefit from religion. The truth is that religion awakens the thinking capacity in man. If religion is accepted as a means of intellectual awakening, human life will be revolutionized.

The reason terrorists are surfacing from within religious circles is that religion has degenerated into stagnant rituals. The thinking of religious people is not being shaped by religion; rather it is being formed by other factors like national and communal interests, which have nothing to do with religion. As we know, national and communal interests always produce negative thinking within man. Therefore, if we want to change this situation, we must revive religion's true form. The source of this true form of religion is not a concept or a group, but the divine teachings.

24

Islam and Modern Science

The extraordinary success achieved by the mujahidin movement is in large measure due to its having received widespread support of Muslims. If its votaries had not been confident that their community was by their side, they would have been discouraged to the point of allowing the movement to die a natural death. Indeed, it is the factor of widespread and constant public support which has enabled the terrorists to continue their destructive activities with such audacity. This is no simple matter and has to be seen in the light of the Muslim psyche which is common to many Muslims of the present day.

To understand the phenomenon of terrorism in the name of Islam, we will have to understand the Muslims of today, almost all of whom have been living with a pervasive feeling of defeatism. They read in the Quran and the Hadith that Islam is the religion of the Almighty God, which means that it has every right to be the dominant religion. According to a Hadith, Islam has come to the world to dominate and not be dominated.[1] When Prophet Muhammad was asked what jihad was, he replied that it was a struggle to ensure that God's word reigned supreme.[2]

Therefore, while the Muslim mind of today dwells on the fact that Islam is a religion of dominance, it remains oppressed by the reality that currently Islam is in a state of subjugation. When on 11 September 2001 the terrorists managed to demolish a prominent symbol of grandeur of the country Muslims regarded as the number one enemy of Islam, many Muslims rejoiced in the belief that its perpetrators had been specially sent by God to revive the glory of Islam. Muslims saw in them champions of the cause of Islam, whose actions challenged Islam's greatest enemy. As such, they gladly offered them their full support.

But the truth is that all such sentiments are nothing more than baseless wishful thinking. Terrorism has nothing to do with Islam and it is certainly not through any terrorist action that the word of Islam will ever reign supreme.

The point where Muslims went wrong goes back to the eighteenth century. For about a thousand years, the major part of the known world had been ruled by Muslims who enjoyed the status of a single superpower. However, in the wake of the Renaissance, the Western nations grew in power and Muslim empires and kingdoms lost their territories and their supremacy. These included the kingdom of Andalusia in Spain, the Ottoman empire in Turkey and the Mughal empire in India. After the Second World War, Muslim countries did attain political freedom, but this freedom again amounted to little more than economic slavery.

The end of Muslim empires in modern times saw the beginning of misguided thinking on the part of Muslims, which culminated in the form of violent terrorism. Muslim leaders at that stage took the political decline of Muslims to be the equivalent of Islam declining as a religion. In fact, the two were not related at all.

The decline of the Muslim empires in modern times was, in reality, the decline of certain Muslim dynasties, and not in any way related to the decline of Islam. This did undoubtedly take place after the rise of Western civilizations, but it must not be linked to the decline of Muslim polity. Had it had anything to do with political decline, it would by now have ceased to exist altogether. After the Second World War, Muslims found themselves once again in a position to establish independent Muslim states. As of today, there are about fifty-seven Muslim states in the world, but even so they have not been able to halt the process of the ideological decline of Islam.

The cause of such a decline goes far deeper than the cause of Islam's political decline. To have a proper appreciation of the true nature of this matter, we have to bear in mind the course of Islamic history.

Islam took root in AD 610. A monotheistic religion, it came at a time when polytheistic culture, enjoying the political support of the rulers of the time, prevailed in every country. Therefore, an inevitable battle had to be fought between monotheism and polytheism. The early Muslims had to make all kinds of sacrifices to meet the challenge of polytheism (shirk), until the period of confrontation finally came to an end, paving the way for the age of monotheism.

History tells us that the age of monotheism lasted for about a thousand years, during which time polytheism never posed a powerful challenge to it. But in the Middle Ages, the European Renaissance, with its literary, artistic and scientific revival, gave rise to the kind of thinking which led to atheism. The new scientific thinking was used to support atheism, and to dismiss religion, including Islam, as products of superstition. Although science, the science of nature, is neither religious nor irreligious, atheism steadily emerged as a new and formidable rival. This trend began markedly in the sixteenth century and, in the space of a few centuries, it became thoroughly entrenched as an intellectual discipline. Over the last two hundred years, hundreds of books have been written on this subject.

'Scientific' atheism spread very fast until it came to dominate all branches of learning. Apparently, it offered proof, by means of arguments developed in the twentieth century, that God did not exist, revelation was not real, no book was a sacred book, and that Paradise and Hell were merely concocted stories.

This trend of modern scientific thinking began with Sir Isaac Newton. After that, one after another, numerous prominent scientists lent conviction to atheism through their research. None of these scientists was himself an atheist, but the thinking produced by their research indirectly supported the atheistic concept.

For instance, Newton and other scientists showed that a principle of causation is at work behind all the events taking place in the world. In ancient times—an age of superstition—man regarded nature as something mysterious. Thus every natural event was believed to be supernatural. But when science discovered material reasons behind these events, it came to be believed consciously or unconsciously that they did not take place at the instigation of God, but could be traced to purely physical causes. Therefore, modern atheist thinkers like Julian Huxley have claimed:

'If events are due to natural causes, they are not due to supernatural causes.'[3]

This atheism that rose on the strength of science was responsible for the situation which was interpreted as subjugation of the Islamic religion. People in general began to doubt the existence of God. Islam did not appear to them as a religion of the scientific age. From their changed viewpoint, the very veracity of religion became suspect.

That the decline of the Muslim empires began at the same time as doubts were being cast on the ideological veracity of Islam was a matter of pure coincidence. In no way did the ideological decline of Islam result from the political decline of the Muslim empire. But because of the contemporaneity of these happenings, almost all the Muslim thinkers of this period were victims of misunderstanding of their own history. Without reviewing the matter in depth, they came to hold that the political decline of the Muslims was responsible for the ideological decline of Islam. Having arrived at this wrong conclusion, they started a political jihad all over the world. In both Muslim and non-Muslim countries, movements were launched to regain political power for the Muslims. All of their promoters believed that so long as Muslims were bereft of political power Islam could never secure a dominant position.

They failed to understand that the dominance of the word of Islam meant the ideological dominance of truth, whereas Muslim political power only meant the political rule of a community or a family. Today, after two hundred years of political jihad, the dominance of Islam is yet to become a reality. Throughout this long period of two hundred years, right from Tipu Sultan of Mysore (d. 1799) to Yasser Arafat of Palestine (d. 2005), Muslims have made huge sacrifices in terms of lives and property, so that Islam regains its position of dominance. But all these sacrifices during this period, considered to exceed even all those made over the rest of 1400 years of Islam's total existence, have been in vain. When, in the wake of the Second World War, Muslims established more than fifty independent states, the question of the dominance of Islam still remained an unrealized dream.

Therefore, the subjugation of Islam in the present day has to be seen as ideological in nature. The reason for this subjugation is that Islam has not received the academic and ideological support which is its due. Its former spell of dominance can be regained only when such support of scientific argument is generated and measures up to the standard of modern times.

Islam's dominance in the early stages was not the result of Muslim political supremacy, but was rather the outcome of its own ideological strength. As we know, during the period of the Abbasid caliphate, Muslims studied the sciences and were in the vanguard of intellectual inquiry. The books that were available at that time was translated into Arabic and it was reviewed on a large scale. To disseminate the sciences, Muslims set up the largest institution of learning ever established in those times—the Muslim University of Cordova.

The history of Islam is long and many books have been written on it. A notable example is Professor Hitti's book, *The History of Arabs*, which tells us that the Muslims of early times, having made the literature in every discipline available, provided a philosophical description of Islam, which enabled them to establish its ideological veracity. This task was so successfully accomplished that not only did Islamic ideology become understandable to the contemporary mind, but the academic community could in no way refute the validity of the religion.

The natural sciences developed in the early period of Islam—mostly of a speculative and philosophical nature—were based on the ancient Greek form of reasoning known as syllogism. Muslims absorbed the Greek logic, and the deductive formula which it offered was made to serve as an intellectual support, to the point where, academically, no room was left for the veracity of Islam to be refuted.

But after the emergence of modern science, the state of affairs changed totally. Modern science demolished the ancient form of logic based on supposition and replaced it with the new scientific logic. While ancient Greek philosophy was based on speculation, modern scientific logic based itself on facts.

This difference of approach tempered the influence of antiquity, thus bringing to an end the age which had provided an academic base for Islamic ideology. The reason for the subjugation of the word of Islam was the demolition of a congenial ideological base, rather than the setting at naught of a political base.

When the scientific revolution ushered in a modernity of thought, the need was felt to give fresh momentum to the academic activities which had been so vibrant during the Abbasid caliphate. Now it became essential for Muslim scholars to study modern thought, to understand it well, and then to strive to establish anew Islam's ideological base on modern scientific lines—just as Muslim scholars had done in the early days. But unfortunately, this could not be done in time to stem the tide of anti-Islamic thinking. The reason for this was that almost all the scholars of this period failed to differentiate between Muslim rule and Islamic ideology.

The lack of proper awareness made Muslims regard the ideological decline of Islam as the result of their own political decline. That is why they engaged themselves in fighting against Western nations on the political front. To them, it was these very nations that were at the root of the Muslim political failure. Launching themselves on this course of action, which was a matter of extreme gravity, was as ill-judged and wrongly directed as giving energy-booster injections to a person who had not been able to have an education. Improved health, while of great value in itself, can hardly be a substitute for education.

Another mistake of equal gravity was made when, due to their political resentment of Western nations, Muslim scholars and leaders began to demonstrate their abhorrence for the language and sciences of the West. They made every attempt to keep their Muslim brethren away from Western education so that their faith might be preserved. They failed to understand that the issue at hand was not simply about safeguarding Islam, but rather about establishing a new scientific basis for it. Depriving Muslims at large of the awareness that they had to strive towards formulating a strong scientific basis for Islam was a major step in the wrong direction.

Islam is a manifestation of exactly the same universal law according to which, as demonstrated by science, the entire universe functions. Islam is a religion of nature. It remains eternally alive, just like the sun. Any cloud can temporarily veil the brightness of the sun, but no sooner does the cloud disappear than the sun emerges, bright and shining as earlier.

The traditional interpretation of Islam in the modern scientific age is like veiling the sun. Once Islam receives scientific argument in its support, it will shine bright like the sun once again. During the age of Newton the world of scientific research was limited to what was called the macro world. In those times, it was held that all the things of the world, in their ultimate analysis, were a combination of atoms and the atom was something which could be weighed and measured.

In the light of this theory, it was held that only those things which could be weighed and measured or were tangible had any real existence. The consensus was that anything which fell into any other category had no real existence. This meant that only the direct argument was scientifically valid.

But in the era of Einstein when the atom was split, a revolutionary event took place. In his time, human knowledge extended in scope, from the macro to the micro world. Now it was demonstrated that the atom was not the ultimate building block, being composed as it is of electrons and protons. Further research showed that the electron was not a material particle like the atom, but was rather intangible waves or energy which could not be seen. It could be apprehended only by means of its indirect effect, or by inference. Therefore unobservable things that could be proved through inference also came to be considered as having a real existence.

In making the correlation between sub-atomic particles and wave motion, a major hurdle was surmounted. This could be done only by the method of inference and the greatest result of this was that the inferential method now rested on a solid scientific base. Finally, it was accepted that an inferential argument was as valid as a direct argument.

This change in logic revolutionized the world of science. In the pre-Einstein days, it was held that religion had only secondary arguments at its disposal, and that in religion primary argument was untenable. Since all arguments on religion and Islamic beliefs were of an inferential nature and, by the former definition, inference had been relegated to the position of secondary argument, religion was included in those sciences which were described as speculative.

But after the splitting of the atom, inferential argument was elevated to the level of scientific argument. Consequently, the scientific base of the Islamic religion also changed. Now the method of religious, or inferential argument, ranked as primary rather than as secondary argument.

Later, many new developments took place in the field of human knowledge. For instance, under the influence of the first phase of science, the British writer Julian Huxley wrote a book which set forth that man was no longer in need of God as he was now able to manage all his affairs on his own. This book was called *Man Stands Alone* (1941). However, an American, Cressy Morrison, published a book which, in the light of scientific facts, took a contrary stand and proved that man, as a mere creature, could never enjoy the status of an omnipotent God. This book was titled *Man Does Not Stand Alone* (1944).

In his book *Why I Am Not a Christian* (1927), Bertrand Russell wrote that the argument from design used to prove the existence of God, although purportedly scientific in conception, had nevertheless been demolished by Darwinism. In an answer to this book, Professor Arnold Lunn wrote *Revolt against Reason* (1950). This book showed how a concept, in itself not really established—in this instance, Darwinism—could destroy a well-established concept, that is, argument from design: 'Where there is a design (the universe) there is a designer.'

After the revolutionary change that saw inferential argument being elevated to the level of scientific argument, the distance between religion and science, both being equal aspects of knowledge, began to dwindle rapidly. In this second phase of scientific development, there arose many superior minds who showed, by referring to modern discoveries, that religious truths were as real as material truths.

The first setback to the old Newtonian phase came when Newton's material interpretation of the corpuscular theory of light (that light is made up of small discrete particles called corpuscles) was disproved. This error was detected for the first time when scientists tried to interpret light in material terms. The great efforts made to explain the material nature of light led to the concept of ether, which was quite abstract and an unestablished element. Yet, this strange concept continued to be in circulation for some generations. But the difficulties became ever more insurmountable with new scientific discoveries. Then came the publication of Maxwell's demonstration that light was an electromagnetic phenomenon. It had finally dawned on men of science that there was, after all, nothing sacrosanct about Newtonian entities. After a certain amount of hesitation, and a few desperate efforts to make electricity mechanical, electricity was added to the list of irreducible elements.

This may seem to have been a simple step to take, but it was, in reality, of profound significance. The Newtonian concepts were all of a kind that one seemed to understand intimately. Thus, the mass of a body was the quantity of matter in it. Force was a notion derived from our experience of muscular effort. We supposed that we knew the nature of what we were talking about. But in the case of electricity, its nature was precisely what we did not know. Attempts to represent it in familiar terms, for example, as a condition of strain in the ether, had been given up. All that we knew about electricity was the way it affected our measuring instruments. The precise description of this behaviour gave us the mathematical specification of electricity and this, in truth, was all we knew about it. It is only now, in retrospect, that we can see how very significant a step this was. An entity had been admitted into physics of which we knew nothing but its mathematical structure.

In the realm of the physical science, we have had three major paradigm shifts in the last four centuries. First we had the Newtonian hypothesis that *matter* was the basic building block of the universe. In the early twentieth century, this gave way to the Einsteinian paradigm of *energy* being the basic building block. And the latest is the David Bohm era when more and more scientists are accepting *consciousness* to be the basic building block. And it is obvious that consciousness is only the other name for God.

Thus, in the twentieth century began the spiritualization of science. But by end of the century, we find that superior minds of this kind were not available to further this movement. Probably, the reason for this could be traced to the new societal phenomenon known as consumerism. The extraordinary, worldwide popularity of consumerism gave importance to those things which were marketable. The movement of spiritualization of science was related to theoretical science, upon which no great commercial value could be placed. Therefore, all the superior minds began to work in the field of technology, as all great economic benefits had come to be associated with the technical branches of scientific endeavour. Research in theoretical science came almost to a standstill.

Now, more than ever, there was a need for great religious minds to engage themselves in this task of spiritualization of science and bring it to a satisfactory conclusion. But, unfortunately, this was not to be. There certainly were superior minds in religious circles, but they chose to engage themselves in other activities.

After the emergence of modern civilization, one new problem faced by men of religion was that, under the influence of modern education and modern thought, people started doubting traditional religious beliefs. Therefore, many great religious thinkers devoted themselves to defending their religion. Great minds were produced within Hinduism, one of the most prominent being Dr S. Radhakrishnan. But such thinkers devoted themselves to providing rational proof only of the validity of Hindu religious mythology. Similarly, there arose great minds in Christianity, such as Billy Graham. However, such preachers likewise engaged themselves in providing a rational basis only for traditional Christian beliefs.

Great minds appeared also among Muslims, for instance, Sayyed Jamaluddin Afghani. But Muslim minds strayed from the central task of giving a scientific backing to religion. In exactly the same period that Muslims faced political decline, their intellectuals engaged themselves pointlessly on the political front. Some of them devoted their entire lives to this political battle in the belief that providing Islam with a political interpretation was the most urgent task to be performed. Thus Muslim minds, lost in the jungle of politics, failed to advance the cause of the spiritualization of science.

Indeed, in modern times, the greatest task was to work for the ascendancy of the word of Islam. But this task needed neither armed jihad nor a political interpretation of Islam. Nor did it need terrorists to play a role in this matter. The fact that, in spite of several generations of Muslims making great sacrifices over a period of two hundred years, not even one per cent of the actual goal has been attained is enough proof that such strategies are wrong.

There is no doubt that the greatest problem in present times is that Islam has lost the support of the kind of human knowledge which would have worked in its favour. This support can be summoned up once again only when the process which we have called the spiritualization of science reaches completion. The need of the hour is for superior Muslim minds to devote themselves to this task. Muslims of today do not need activists who hijack planes or choose to become suicide bombers, but rather thinkers such as A.N. Whitehead, Arthur Eddington and James Jeans. Terrorists can play only a destructive role, while what is needed today is positive and constructive action, particularly that which can be carried on along intellectual and scientific lines.

The Quran (2:31) tells us that God gave man knowledge of all the things in the world. Modern discoveries relating to the human brain read like an interpretation of this verse. Modern research tells us that each human brain is made up of countless particles—according to one estimate, more than 100 million, billion billion. These particles are not like sand particles, but more like information particles. It is as if through these particles, God has stocked the human brain with all kinds of information—both physical and spiritual.

Modern scientists, by making new discoveries about the universe, have put at our disposal a huge amount of knowledge. These discoveries are, in fact, not new discoveries as such, but merely the activation of the information particles already present in the human brain. Similarly, man has on a very large scale succeeded in uncovering the physical information fed into his mind. However, so far as the spiritual information fed into the human brain is concerned, a large part of it has yet to be unfolded. This is a task yet to be performed. It is the performance of this task which will pave the way to a peaceful culture as against a conflict culture in the world.

25

Who Is Dajjal?

We learn from the traditions of Prophet Muhammad that a man called Dajjal will be born in the Muslim community.[1] The literal meaning of 'Dajjal' is 'great deceiver'. None but one who speaks in the language of the Quran and the Hadith can attempt to become a great deceiver of Muslims. Therefore, Dajjal would be one who justifies his actions by quoting the Quran and the Hadith, for only a leader who manages to impress upon the people that his actions are governed by Islam can be successful. The second condition warranting his appearance is that he must rise in an age when circumstances perfectly favour him.

The books of Hadith say that Dajjal will appear in the time of Christ, and that Christ will kill Dajjal. This killing cannot be a physical killing in the ordinary sense: it will certainly be an ideological killing. Dajjal will be an ideological evil (fitna) leading—in the name of Islam—to a movement based on hatred and violence, which will be justified by a self-devised interpretation of Islam.[2] On account of this ideology, Muslims will be deceived and will become the supporters of Dajjal. To 'kill' Dajjal, in such a situation, it is necessary that his perverted ideology be proved wrong and his misleading interpretation of Islam be nullified by counter-arguments. We cannot say with certainty who Dajjal or his 'killer' might be. But it is certain that his obliteration will take place when the end of this world draws near. One will certainly appear who plays the role of Dajjal and another will appear who by means of powerful counter-arguments will prove that Dajjal's ideology is false and baseless, and thus put an end to the evil.

A number of traditions have been recorded in the books of the Hadith, which relate to this evil brought about by Dajjal and to the coming of Christ. These traditions have gained wide currency and are taken quite literally, so people are waiting for the day when this monster will appear in human form and win a large number of converts. This will be followed by the coming of Christ who will kill the monster, so that truth and justice may prevail throughout the world.

These traditions have been largely regarded as allegorical. If read literally, they describe the supernatural advent, during the last days of the world, of two major personalities: the negative character Dajjal and the positive character Christ. But according to my research and interpretation, both these personalities will be very much a part of the natural world. And intelligence and common sense alone will be enough to recognize them. Moreover, after delving deeply into this matter, I have come to the conclusion that Dajjal will not be a strange, beast-like creature, but rather a man of intellectual calibre and endowed with great leadership qualities. He will, in fact, be the greatest of those leaders, known as Al-Aimmatul Muzillun,[3] who will mislead the world. Dajjal will have the semblance of a religious person, for if he did not appear as such to the people, he would not be able to win so many converts to his deceptive ideology.

A number of traditions describe Dajjal in a symbolic manner. For instance, we learn from the Hadith that Dajjal will possess a mountain of bread and a river of water.[4] This means that he will appear at a time of great abundance and economic prosperity. Similarly, there is a tradition that Dajjal's voice will be heard from the East to the West.[5] This is a plain reference to the modern age, meaning that Dajjal will come in the era of television and modern communications.

The battle between Dajjal and Christ cannot be taken in a literal sense. Probably, it will be an ideological battle fought in the media arena. That is, Christ will vanquish Dajjal ideologically, proving him wrong and his stand baseless by means of superior arguments, rather than by vanquishing him physically.

Now the question arises as to what Dajjal's particular form of evil (fitna) will be. We learn from the Hadith that the nature of the evil perpetrated by Dajjal will be his dexterity in presenting falsehood in the form of truth. He will present a deceptive picture of Islam to people and be able to convince them it is the truth. In short, he will harbour un-Islamic thoughts, but will portray his thinking as genuinely Islamic and will succeed in convincing the people that what he offers is the true version of Islam.

I have thought deeply over this issue in the light of the traditions. The conclusion I have reached is that the evil (fitna) of Dajjal will be ideological in nature. This will take the shape of projecting Islam not just as a religion but also as a political system.

According to this modern, political interpretation of Islam, it should be the duty of the believers to establish the Kingdom of God on earth, bringing to an end the rule of non-Islamic law all over the world and replacing it with the rule of Islamic law. In other words, the sole aim of Muslims is to raise the political flag of Islam; they are duty-bound to conquer non-Islamic communities and establish the dominance of Islam; the aim of jihad is to establish this universal Islamic government; and so on.

This ideology is, without doubt, the greatest evil (fitna) of modern times. The greatest harm it does is to eternally divide the inhabitants of this earth into two warring groups. One group will fight to gain power, while the other will fight to save itself from being subjugated. This ideology is undoubtedly against the divine scheme of creation, according to which human beings all over the world should be divided into groups of preachers of truth and their audience. These preachers of truth are called *dai* and those to whom the message is preached are referred to as *madu*. The Quran uses the term *shahid* or 'witness' for dai and *mashhud* or 'the witnessed' for madu (85:3).

The preacher, who has nothing but benevolence for his audience in his heart, exhorts his listeners to accept the message of truth in a way which is peaceful, non-political and non-violent.

Projecting Islam in the form of a ruling system is no trivial matter. Attempting to inculcate such a concept is totally against the aims and objectives of Islam and, were this attempt to be successful, it could place the entire scheme of Islam in jeopardy. This would be like killing Islam in the name of Islam.

The inevitable result of political Islam would be that the thinking of those who subscribe to its ideology would be oriented entirely towards politics. Whereas man's thinking—when properly oriented—should centre on God and the Hereafter.

Another kind of harm brought about by this ideology is that it superimposes a political way of thinking upon the mission-oriented thinking that makes man human-friendly and a benefactor. Mission-oriented thinking, after all, is superior to the political way of thinking in that it makes man set his sights on saving God's servants from hellfire and making them deserving of Paradise in the eyes of God. Thus, the interests of a preacher of truth lie not in acquiring political dominance but rather in helping people gain entry into Paradise.

The politicized concept of Islam divides people into two perpetually hostile, clashing groups. The atmosphere of normalcy, which is an essential condition for conducting missionary work, is consequently vitiated by hatred, rivalry and enmity. In all aspects an atmosphere of peace, well-wishing and mutual trust must prevail, if missionary work is to be successful.

Every ideology fosters a world view derived from its core concepts and, accordingly, it shapes human relations.

For instance, the philosophy of Nazism was that the Germans—the Aryans—were racially superior. They were the 'master race'. As such, Nazi Germans developed a feeling of superiority and consequently looked down upon the other races as being inferior. The concept of Islam is based on the principle of propagation of truth. According to this concept, the believers are preachers of truth or dai while non-believers have the status of audience or madu. This concept necessarily inculcates the feeling of benevolence in the minds of the believers for everyone else. Their thinking naturally becomes audience-friendly or human-friendly.

On the other hand, regarding Islam as a political system produces negative thinking to the point where, consciously or unconsciously, the adherent of that system comes to regard himself as the ruler and the others as his subjects. He is engrossed in political activities day in and day out, and devotes himself to worldly politics rather than to issues relating to the Hereafter. Describing God's religion in terms of a 'total system' and holding it to be the believer's duty to strive to implement it in its total form is an extremist concept, which inevitably results in diverting man's attention towards political achievements. He then comes to regard the possession of political power as the greatest goal to strive for. He thinks that, without possessing political power, the desired ruling system cannot be established. In this way, the same evil that characterizes so-called revolutionary parties is produced under the banner of Islam. That is, politics becomes the focus of all theoretical and practical activities, and all other more important aspects, such as spirituality and orientation towards God and the Hereafter, are relegated to the background. This is the inevitable result of describing Islam in terms of a ruling system. In such a situation, people's minds, consciously or unconsciously, are diverted from God and the Hereafter, and their attention is driven towards political activities. Although, in this context, reference is made to spirituality and the God-oriented life, it is only in passing, thus reducing them to mere formalities.

This version of Islam, focused as it is on political thinking, is almost bereft of God-oriented thinking. It engages in political confrontation, but has no element of sympathy for human beings. It produces the mentality of seeing others only as rivals, so that they cannot be seen as friends. It breeds a jungle of hatred, not an orchard of love. It gives preference to worldly activities while the heart and the mind are devoid of the remembrance of God.

There is great harm in this political version of Islam. One major negative point of this ideology is that it puts the believer severely to the test by loading him with a responsibility which is beyond normal human capacity and which God does not expect him to take up at all. If this ideology is to be believed, the believers have only two choices in this world—either they destroy themselves by clashing with the rulers or else lead a life of hypocrisy by making compromises with them.

According to this political concept, the objective of Islam is to rule the world. It glorifies this rule as 'divine' and brands all other systems as 'satanic'. It further qualifies these other systems as unlawful for the believers—they are thus duty-bound to fight such systems and to exert themselves to bring about their downfall. They are not ready to think of trying to reach a compromise with them. Muslims must go on fighting such systems, generation after generation, even if their lives are destroyed in the process.

The other alternative open to the believers is to compromise with the 'satanic' system, as they call it. But to their mind, to build their lives under this system would be totally hypocritical. A movement that is based on the concept of replacing 'satanic' rule with 'divine' rule comes into conflict mostly with two kinds of political powers: one, the secular rule of non-Muslims; and the other, corrupt Muslim rule. According to this ideology, fighting the secular rule of non-Muslims is necessary so that divine rule may be established in its place. And fighting corrupt Muslim rule becomes a duty when it is seen that the Muslims in power are not themselves leading Islamic lives and are neither obeying nor enforcing divine laws. Thus, according to the contrived political concept of Islam, fighting with both types of rulers is obligatory. But we have already proved that when judged by the actual teachings of the Quran, this kind of war is undoubtedly an unlawful (haram) act. No such war is allowed in Islam.

As regards any non-Muslim community or any non-Muslim government, the duty of the believers is only one: to convey to them the message of monotheism, to exhort them to follow the path of Paradise and shun the path of Hell. Under no circumstances is any other attitude lawful for them. Fighting a non-Muslim government is lawful for a Muslim government only if done in defence, where there has been a clear case of aggression. No war save a defensive one is lawful in Islam. So far as fighting Muslim rulers is concerned, that is also unlawful, according to the teachings of Islam. A number of traditions have been recorded where Prophet Muhammad has forbidden his followers to wage war with Muslim rulers in the name of reform, even when those rulers have been found guilty of perversion. According to the traditions, Muslims can only give words of advice rather than wage war in the name of reform.[6] Waging war with Muslim rulers is nothing less than armed revolt (*khuruj*), and revolt is unlawful. There is no concept of war for the purpose of reform in Islam. Thus fighting a violent jihad against both Muslim and non-Muslim rulers is unlawful. The responsibility of the believers as regards non-Muslim rulers is that of peacefully carrying the mission of truth to them.

The teaching of a non-confrontational approach as regards Muslim rulers is based on profound wisdom. The truth is that corruption in rulers never closes the door on conducting peaceful mission and reform. Despite the imperfections of the Muslim rulers, many vistas remain open for peaceful activities.

Today, with the sphere of political power having been greatly narrowed down, this possibility is greater than ever before. It has become possible to do many kinds of constructive work—such as preaching of Islam, spreading education, carrying out social welfare and reform activities, and developing character in individuals. All these activities can be pursued outside the political sphere, and are all the more effectively performed through the establishment of educational and other such institutions. Moreover, freedom of speech and modern communications have greatly extended the sphere of these activities. In these circumstances, the importance and utility of propagating the correct teachings of Islam have greatly increased.

The truth is that now there is no longer any need to clash with governments. All those improvements which could earlier be achieved only with the support of political power can be now achieved without it. Hence, there is no need to strive for political power, which in any case should never be an issue in Islam. The theory of political Islam simply does not exist in the Quran. That is a theory which has been concocted and popularized by the deliberate misrepresentation of the Quran. For example, verse 40, chapter 12, uses the word *hukm* to refer to supernatural power which belongs only to God. But hukm is commonly misinterpreted as political power. (The verses quoted in support of this theory have been analysed in a separate chapter.)

26

An Abode of Peace

The period of the Pious Caliphate (AD 632–661) followed
upon the death of the Prophet in AD 632. The Pious
Caliphate was succeeded by the Umayyads (AD 661–750).
Their successors, the Abbasids, reigned from AD 750 to AD
1258, during which period Islamic law (fiqh) was developed
and compiled as a discipline.

The terms *Darul Islam*, *Darul Harb* and *Darul Kufr* (the
Abode of Islam, the Abode of War and the Abode of Deniers)
do not occur in the Quran or the Hadith. They were coined
for the first time by Muslim jurists during the Abbasid
period. According to this terminology, the world was divided
into two large regions. The part of the world ruled by
Muslims was called Darul Islam. The rest of the world ruled
by others was called Darul Kufr or Darul Harb (the Land
of Kafirs or the Land of War). For the Muslims, there were
therefore these two distinct spheres of influence: the land
of Islam, which meant the land where Muslims had full
freedom to practise their religion; and the land of war, which
meant the place where Muslims had no such freedom. The
land of war indicated those areas of the world where Muslims

found themselves in unfavourable circumstances and war was always imminent. The jihad of the present-day Muslims is, in fact, a legacy of this early, potentially unstable situation.

As a result of this division worked out by Islamic law, Muslims have come to feel, consciously or unconsciously, that they are always in danger in those countries where they are not in a position of power, and that a war with non-Muslims could be in the offing at any time. According to this division, Darul Harb was in effect the *Dar al Aada* (the Land of Enemies). That is why the idea took root in the minds of the Muslims that those potential enemies should be fought and subjugated, so that they were no longer a threat to them.

Muslim thinking continued along these lines for over a period of a thousand years. The present-day Muslims have had some bitter experiences at the hands of some nations, which led them to think that their enemies have rallied and united against them. This idea has come to be so firmly entrenched in the Muslim psyche that a certain section of Muslims have started an armed jihad on the grounds that all nations other than Muslim nations are the enemies of Islam.

The whole problem is simply the creation of early Muslim jurists and has nothing to do with the tenet of Islam. Islam is an eternal religion, but the ever-present factor of time inherent in this or similar problems must also be taken into account, for cultural and social circumstances inevitably change with the times; Islam makes provision for this too. That is why there is a legal principle in Islam that social directives must be modified to be in tune with altered circumstances. And that is also why periodically the need for a reapplication of Islam's eternal teachings is strongly felt. In Islam, the reasoned approach to taking such a step is termed 'ijtihad' or 'tajdeed'.

There is a Hadith which tells us that every hundred years a mujaddid or renewer will be born in the Muslim community.[1] This means that time is a changing reality—one period comes to an end, to make room for another. In such circumstances, each new generation feels the need for a religion's revival. The task of revival does not mean reform or revision. It simply means being instrumental in reapplying Islamic principles to changed circumstances.

Studies show the great differences between the circumstances of the Abbasid period and of the present age. In the circumstances prevailing during the Abbasid period, the terms Darul Islam and Darul Harb could have been relevant; but in today's circumstances, they no longer apply. Therefore, there is an urgent need for these terms to be relegated to the shelves of historical archives and for new terms to be evolved which meet the exigencies of new situations.

In the seventh century AD, at the time of the advent of Islam, the entire world was dominated by the scourge of religious coercion. The official religion of a country had to be adopted by its people—any other religion was unacceptable. Thus, whenever anyone chose to follow any religion other than the state religion, he did so at the risk of religious persecution. It was against this background that the jurists of the Abbasid period devised such terms as Darul Islam, Darul Kufr and Darul Harb.

After the seventh century, with the spread of Islam, human society was revolutionized. One aspect of the changes wrought by the Islamic revolution was the outlawing of religious persecution so that religious freedom could be enjoyed. This change was not a development which could be brought about in a very short period of time. Rather, it was a gradual ongoing process, which culminated centuries later in the European Renaissance. This intellectual reawakening brought about far-reaching changes in Europe after the sixteenth century, and one of its main aspects was that religious freedom came to be held as an absolute human right, whatever the situation. If, in earlier times, Muslims had to practise their religion in defiance of, or under the dire threat of, religious coercion, in modern times they had ample opportunities to follow their religion in an atmosphere of complete religious freedom. So, what had formerly been possible only in Darul Islam, now became equally possible in Darul Harb and Darul Kufr.

This denotes a sea change in present-day circumstances, which calls for a revision of the terms of the Abbasid period to bring them in line with the latest developments. Man formulates his thoughts with the help of words. If he is not given words relevant to his situation, he will lose his moral bearings. Now, with the altered situation, as far as religious freedom is concerned, the whole world is Darul Islam. The circumstances that necessitated the world's division into two separate categories no longer exist. After the establishment of religious freedom on a global scale, the entire world has become one, and now only the phrase of *Darul Amn* (the Abode of Peace) or *Darul Insan* (the Abode of Human Beings) may properly be applied to it.

The expressions Darul Harb and Darul Kufr were coined during the Abbasid period and not during the early phase of Islam. Now the time has come to abandon them totally. Even the expression Darul Islam should be dispensed with, given that this term was a latter-day innovation. After the emigration of the Prophet, when the first Muslim city state was established in Madinah, it was simply called Madinah and not Darul Islam. After the conquest of Makkah, Muslim rule was established all over Arabia, but it was still not given the name of Darul Islam. Subsequently, Muslim governments were established in Damascus, Cairo, Baghdad and Cordova, but these Muslim countries were never called Darul Islam. It is only in present times that certain Muslim countries applied this name to themselves.

This being so, it is essential that every country be called by its original name and no new appellations invented for it. When one country is given the name Darul Islam and the rest of the countries are referred to as a kind of war zone, it gives rise to the concept of 'us' and 'them'. Such a mentality is a major obstacle to the development of a nation, for true progress is inevitably the result of thinking which is universal rather than regional in nature.

27

The Gifts from the West

The Quran repeatedly declares:

> 'He has subjected whatever is in heaven and is on the earth to you.' (45:13)

This means that all things in the heavens and on the earth have been made to serve man. But to derive benefit from these things, their latent powers have to be discovered and then harnessed to fulfil human needs.

Although nature's bounty was stressed in the Quran, the discoverers of this bounty were the people of the West. It was they who realized its potential. Muslim nations have had no share either in this discovery or in the harnessing of nature's resources.

As the Quran puts it:

> 'He has given you all that you asked of him.' (14:34)

The blessings of God mentioned in this verse are of two kinds. The first kind comprises those blessings which already existed on the earth from the day man set foot there, for instance, animals, water, air and light. Other kinds of blessings are those which were not yet in existence at the time of the revelation of the Quran, for instance, industrial machinery, railways, motorcars, aeroplanes, telephones and electricity.

The second kinds of things were invented mostly by the West, but today they are in general use everywhere.

The Quran tells us that God's signs are hidden in the heavens and in human souls (41:53). In modern times, these signs have come into full view through scientific discoveries and have established the veracity of God's religion.[1] But this task too was performed by the West. Muslims regularly avail themselves of the resulting facilities, but they had no share in bringing them into existence.

The Prophet predicted that the message of Islam would spread to all homes, whether large or small, all over the world.[2] In the age of the printing press and modern communications, this has become entirely possible. But it was the people of the West who dedicated their lives to realizing and harnessing nature's hidden potential.

It was the Muslims' responsibility to do their utmost to safeguard the Quran. They made elaborate arrangements for this purpose for over a period of a thousand years, memorizing the divine revelations and preparing handwritten copies of them with meticulous precision. But it was only after the invention of the printing press that the Quran attained the state of preservation which would last for all eternity. It was the people of the West who invented the printing press, which is now used also by Muslims.

In earlier times, only traditional arguments could be put forward to prove the veracity of Islamic belief but now, as a result of the modern scientific revolution, it has become possible to present Islamic beliefs in terms of those very arguments which are employed by the scientific world. Thus the people of the West brought into existence a new age of scientific reasoning which enabled the veracity of Islam to be established at the level of the accepted criteria of the modern scientific world. In this too, Muslims played no part.

Moreover, for the first time in human history, the age of total religious freedom has been ushered in. It has become possible to work for the cause of Islam freely, without any obstacle.

The concept of religious freedom was introduced by the Islamic revolution as early as the seventh century AD. It had the effect of changing the course of history. However, the promulgation of this idea and its acceptance was a very gradual process, which reached its culmination only in the nineteenth century. Now, at last, we are living in an age when the concept of religious freedom has become an established fact. This historical change is a great blessing for Islam. But it was the people of the West who were mainly responsible for this development. In this respect, they are not so much the enemies of Muslims as they are their benefactors.

Similarly, the West has given many other boons to Muslims. For instance, the age earlier was characterized by dictatorship or theocracy. It was the West which replaced these systems with the secular form of government. In the secular system, Muslims found an equal place, just like other communities and groups. This was a unique blessing in that they were entitled to all social rights without having to be the rulers. The positive aspects of the present age are all contributions of the West.

The many benefits that Muslims have received from the West are evident in academic, scientific, social and political fields. As a result, Muslims should have been grateful to the West. Owing to their ignorance of the origins of their good fortune, Muslims developed a hatred for the West which led them to violence. Islam, however, does not permit this kind of extremism.

One of the sayings of Prophet Muhammad is worth quoting here:

'One who is not grateful to man cannot be grateful to God.'[3]

In this instance, gratitude means acknowledgement. Acknowledgement is a feeling of the heart. If you drop dye in a glass of water, all of the water will take on the colour of the dye. It is just not possible that one half of the glass of water changes colour while the other half remains uncoloured. The same is true of thankfulness or acknowledgement. If the feeling of thankfulness exists in the heart of an individual, it will become part of his entire personality. It is not possible for him to be thankful in one matter and ungrateful in another.

This saying of Prophet Muhammad is like a warning. It means that if you receive certain benefits from human beings, but do not acknowledge them, it will turn into a very serious issue—it will be a sign that you are not grateful to God either. In such a situation, even if you do utter words of thankfulness to God, it will be mere lip service. To put it in religious terminology, it will be sheer hypocrisy and, as such, a great evil. Indeed, in Islam, there is no evil greater than hypocrisy.

Keeping this caveat in view, it would be no overstatement to say that acknowledging the gifts of the West is a matter of utmost importance, for it concerns the interests of Muslims themselves. If Muslims acknowledge the positive aspects of the West in this matter, they will be credited with thankfulness in the Hereafter, but if they fail to do so they will be held to be ungrateful servants of God. And no God worshipper, in the true sense, can afford to figure as an ingrate in the eyes of his Maker.

28

The Problem of Palestine

The present history of Palestine begins in 1948 in the days of the British empire when Palestine was divided under the terms of the Balfour Declaration. According to this division, less than half of the land of Palestine was given for settlement to the Jews of the Diaspora and more than half was given to the Arabs who inhabited that land.

The Jews were given this right between the first and second world wars under the limited quota system. The expansion of Israel which took place later on was not the result of the Balfour Declaration, but was the outcome of the wrong policy followed by the Arabs.

For instance, the unilateral termination of the lease of the Suez Company in 1956, which in any case was going to expire in 1968 according to the pact, naturally had grave consequences. The selling of land to the Jews by the Palestinian Arabs at high prices had similar results.

Who are the Jews or Israelis? They are the descendants of the Israelites, the progeny of Prophet Jacob and grandsons of Prophet Abraham. To be more specific, the Jews of today are the descendants of Juda, the fourth son of Prophet

Jacob (also known as Israel, which in Hebrew means 'God's servant').

The history of Abraham goes back four thousand years. Abraham had two sons, Ishmael and Isaac. Ishmael, the elder, was the son of Hagar, and Isaac, the younger, was the son of Sara. By the command of God, Abraham settled Ishmael in Arabia and Isaac in Palestine. Isaac had a son called Jacob. He was also called Israel, the progenitor of the Children of Israel. Thus Palestine came to be the homeland of Israelities, just as Arabia came to be the homeland of the Ishmaelites.

As the Jewish religion is based on race, there is no concept of conversion to Judaism. Due to the purity of this race, in direct line from its ancestors, Isaac and Jacob, the common land of all Jews, regardless of which part of the world they inhabit, is Palestine. The homeland of the Ishmaelites was always and still is Arabia. Both were settled in these lands by the command of God.

The ancient times were marked by intolerance in religious matters, which meant that the Jews had to face unpleasant experiences repeatedly. Over the centuries, wave after wave of them left Palestine, their homeland, in large numbers to go into exile. It is this spread of Jews living outside Palestine which is called the Diaspora. It was under the Balfour Declaration that it was decided that the Jews who were living in the Diaspora would return to Palestine.

After 1948, when a number of these Jews who were living in different countries came to Palestine, the Arabs demonstrated a strong negative reaction to them. The greatest organization of Arabs, Al-Ikhwan al-Muslimun, was, in fact, formed as a consequence of these hostile feelings for the Jews. At that time the slogan of the Arab leaders was 'We will drive the Jews into the sea'.

The settlement was strenuously opposed by Arab and non-Arab Muslim leaders alike, to the point where the entire Muslim world had turned against the Jews. All kinds of violence, including suicide bombing, were held to be lawful against them. But all these activities targeting the Jews proved to be counterproductive. The direct loss resulting from these activities was as acutely felt by the Muslims as by the Jews in Palestine, and Muslims all over the world shared indirectly in this loss.

This anti-Jewish policy followed by the Arab and non-Arab Muslims clearly went against Islamic teachings. Under the Balfour Declaration, the division of Palestine was intended to facilitate the return of the Jews in the Diaspora to their own homeland, and this is clearly in accordance with the teachings of the Quran. According to the Quran, the Jews in the time of Prophet Moses were directed by God:

'O my people! Enter the holy land which God has assigned to you.' (5:21)

Who were the Jews of those times? They were those who were living in the Sinai desert in the Diaspora. The 'Holy Land' in this verse refers to Palestine. This verse was addressed to Prophet Moses' contemporaries, the Jews who were living outside Palestine. The words of the Quran 'which God has assigned to you' means that this return to Palestine was to be exactly in accordance with the law of nature. For, according to this law, any individual or group living in exile has the right to return to his or its original homeland.

Abraham had settled one branch of his family in Palestine. Joseph, Jacob's son, was also born into this family. Destined by circumstances to reach Egypt, he was ultimately given a high post in the government of the country by the reigning king (one of the Hiksos dynasty), who was impressed by his capabilities.

After his position was consolidated in Egypt, Joseph invited his family, including his father Jacob, to leave Palestine for Egypt. Once settled in Egypt, his people multiplied and gradually became a powerful racial group in the country of their adoption.

In the years following Joseph's ascendancy, a political revolution in Egypt put in place a new dynasty which supplanted the Hiksos kings. They adopted the title 'Pharaoh'. It was under these new rulers that the Israelites were subjected to oppression, until the advent of Moses, who succeeded in leading the Israelites out of Egypt into the Sinai desert. This was the first stage of their journey. The second stage of their journey was to enter Palestine and settle there in their former homeland.

During the time of Moses, that is, in the time of the ancient Jewish Diaspora, the plan for these exiled Jews to return to their former homeland was made at the behest of God. In modern times, the plan for the return of the exiled Jews of the Diaspora was executed in terms of the Balfour Declaration.

The Problem of the Return to the First Qibla

Muslims in general regard the present problem of Palestine as that concerning the return to the first qibla. They point out that when Prophet Muhammad built a mosque in Madinah and laid down that five prayers had to be ritually recited in it, he followed the Jewish tradition in making al-Masjid al-Aqsa his qibla for a period of sixteen months.

However, this is a misunderstanding. When Muslims migrated to Madinah, they actually worshipped at the direction of the Dome of the Rock (Qubbat al-Sakhra), the Jewish qibla and not at the direction of Al-Masjid al-Aqsa.

At the end of this sixteen-month period, the command was revealed in the Quran to change the qibla. So the Prophet adopted the Kabah as the permanent qibla in accordance with God's command. Referring to this incident, Muslims claim that the problem of Palestine is one of the return to the first qibla. Thus they make the point that this problem is not a national but religious issue for the Muslims. This concept is based entirely on a misunderstanding. The first qibla has nothing to do with al-Masjid al-Aqsa. The name al-Masjid al-Aqsa in the following verse of the Quran has not been cited in the sense of a particular mosque.

'Holy is He who took His servant by night from the sacred place of worship [at Makkah] to the remote house of worship [at Jerusalem]—the precincts of which We have blessed.' (17:1)

The above verse just means a place of worship situated at a distance. It is called the farthest place of worship, because it was situated at a distance of 765 miles from Makkah. Al-Masjid al-Aqsa, in this context, refers to the Jewish place of worship, that is, the Haykal Synagogue.

This Jewish synagogue, built by Solomon in 957 BC, was razed to the ground in 586 BC by the king of Babylonia, Nebuchadnezzar II. After a long period of time, the Jews rebuilt their place of worship. This was again reduced to ruins in AD 70 by the Romans. At present only one wall of the building is left. This is called the 'wailing wall' or the 'western wall'. At the time of the revelation of the Quran, there was no building here; it was only a vacant site. In AD 638, in the time of the second caliph, Umar Farooq, the Muslims entered Jerusalem. Caliph Umar did not have any structure erected on this site. During the Umayyad rule, Caliph Abdul Malik bin Marwan (d. 705) had the present al-Masjid al-Aqsa built in AD 688.

There is another building in the campus of al-Masjid al-Aqsa, which is called the Dome of the Rock (Qubbat al-Sakhra). The sacred rock of the Jews has been situated there since ancient times. It was on this sacred rock that Caliph Abdul Malik ibn Marwan built the present dome in AD 688. It was this sacred rock or Dome of the Rock, the qibla of the Jews, which was made the Muslim qibla temporarily by Prophet Muhammad after his emigration to Madinah. It is this Dome of the Rock that is known as al-Quds and, by extension, this entire area of Jerusalem is called al-Quds.

Muslims in general regard al-Masjid al-Aqsa as the first qibla, and it has become a symbol of the Palestinian struggle. But the mosque has nothing to do with the first qibla. If there is any first qibla, it is the Dome of the Rock rather than al-Masjid al-Aqsa. Furthermore, when Prophet Muhammad was in Makkah, he used to say his prayers after turning in the direction of the Kabah. After his emigration, for about sixteen months, he said his prayers in the direction of the Dome of the Rock. Afterwards, in obedience to God's command, he again started saying his prayers in the direction of the Kabah. In this respect, the Dome of the Rock is the middle qibla and not the first.

In the light of this fact, the expression 'return to the first qibla' is totally without meaning. If this supposed return is attributed to al-Masjid al-Aqsa, it should be noted that it never was the qibla of Prophet Muhammad. At the time of the Hijrah (AD 622), there was only a vacant site there on which a Jewish synagogue had previously stood. There was no mosque in existence at the time of the Prophet. So far as the Dome of the Rock is concerned, there is no question of its return. It was the Jewish qibla earlier and it is the Jewish qibla today. The demand for the return of the Dome of the Rock is as invalid as the demand (if there is any such demand) of the polytheists to return the Kabah to them, as at one time it housed their deities.

When the exiled Jews started coming to Palestine to be settled there, in the wake of the Balfour Declaration of 1948, the only reaction from the Arabs was violent jihad. The Arab countries started funding the Palestinian Arabs on a large scale. They wanted to crush the Jewish state, but they totally failed to achieve their objective.

This was undoubtedly a great mistake on the part of the Arab leaders. Had these Arab leaders learned any lesson from Islamic history, they would have certainly found that there was a better option before them. That was to welcome those Jews as their neighbours and work for the progress and development of Palestine in collaboration with them. These Jews, coming mainly from Western countries, were highly educated, had great expertise in modern science and technology, and as such had the ability to become the best partners the Arabs could hope for so far as the progress and development of Palestine was concerned. But in their welter of emotion, the Arab leaders failed to understand this positive aspect of the matter.

There were very fine examples in the history of Islam of this collaboration between the Jews and the Muslims. When Muslim empires were being established, Muslims undertook the task of translating into Arabic ancient books available in Greek and other languages, which they found in different countries. Translation bureaus were set up and a great number of ancient books were translated under the auspices of institutes such as Bait al-Hikmah, which was established in Baghdad in AD 832, and Dar al-Hikmah, which was set up in Cairo in AD 1005, both under direct state patronage. Later, when the Arabs entered Spain and brought it under their control, they established great academic and educational institutions in Cordoba and Granada where these Arabic translations were rendered into

Latin. These Latin translations were again rendered into different European languages. Not only were translations undertaken but also, side by side, different kinds of research and investigations were carried out on a large scale.

These academic activities led directly to the Renaissance in Europe. In this way, the Muslims of those times acted as a bridge between the ancient traditional age and the modern scientific age.

This fact has been generally acknowledged by Western historians. For instance, acknowledging the contribution of the role of the Arabs, Robert Briffault writes, 'It is highly probable that but for the Arabs, modern industrial civilization would never have arisen at all.'[1]

How did the Arabs perform this great role in the field of learning, especially when no such academic tradition existed among them? The answer is that this feat was achieved by them through their collaboration with others, such as the Christian and Jewish scholars who worked in the institutions established by the Arabs in Iraq, Egypt and Spain. The result of this joint contribution is that grand academic history of medieval times on the basis of which Western Europe made tremendous progress.[2]

In the wake of the Balfour Declaration, a similar opportunity presented itself to the Palestinians, but, blinded by their emotions, their Arab leaders misled them and launched them on the path of confrontation rather than that of collaboration. The Muslim failure to avail of this opportunity put an end to the realization of a great history in the making.

A comparison between the two parts of Palestine—one under Arab rule and the other under Jewish rule—is a telling example of what would have been had the two communities entered into a collaborative exercise. The Jewish-ruled Palestine which, before 1948, was a barren desert has been converted into green fields and orchards. By contrast, the Arab-ruled Palestine is still in the same backward condition as it was prior to 1948. The Palestinians are still waging a futile battle under their unwise leaders. Earlier their goal was to bring Palestine back to its original state, as it was in the pre-1948 period. Now their goal is to bring Palestine to the state of 1967. Meeting both these targets is impossible. This is akin to reversing the course of history and history itself is a witness to the impossibility of such a reversal. The first option for the Palestinians was to willingly accept the status quo of 1948. Now their second option is to accept the present status quo. If they lose this second opportunity as well, they are not going to find a chance to exercise a third option. The third option for them will be death and destruction rather than life and construction.

'Status-quoism' means acceptance of the current situation as it is. This is not a matter of weakness. It is a wise policy of a high order, in accordance with the law of nature. In this world there always exists some controversial issue or the other. Along with this, the very system of nature demands that in every situation there should be opportunities to solve problems. But given the present state of affairs, a result-oriented policy would be to ignore the problems and seize whatever opportunities there may be left for the betterment of the situation. Becoming entangled with controversial issues always comes at the cost of losing such precious opportunities and leaving the situation unimproved.

In Palestine, the Arab leaders have been fighting for their lost land for a long period of time. But if we look at it from the perspective of results, we find that all their efforts and sacrifices have been wasted. Not only have they failed to achieve the target of recovering their land, but they have missed out on precious opportunities to make other kinds of progress, thereby incurring a great loss.

The present age is one of globalization. In the agricultural age of ancient times, land was of the utmost importance; but modern communications have now reduced land to a secondary position. Of prime importance now are the opportunities presenting themselves, thanks to globalization, in equal measure to all. Now anyone working in a modest office can avail of opportunities available the world over. Given this situation, fighting for the acquisition of a piece of land is anachronistic in nature and can never yield positive results.

The present state of affairs in Palestine is a crisis situation, which benefits neither the Arabs nor the Israelis. It is in the interests of both to think seriously, and without prejudice, in order to take some decision to normalize the situation. However, both the parties will have to adopt a realistic approach to the matter. Any condition which is not acceptable to both sides will be unrealistic and will lead to a state of impasse.

As I understand it, the only practicable solution to this problem is for the Arabs to abandon all kinds of terrorism. This is the first prerequisite. Trying to find a solution without fulfilling this condition is to travel in an imaginary world—on a journey which will never reach its destination. So far as Israel is concerned, it will have to give the Palestinian Arabs (residing in Palestine) the same rights as are enjoyed by other residents under the constitution. If both these points are accepted in principle, a practical settlement can be arrived at through peaceful negotiation.

There is much talk about giving land for peace. But on the basis of my knowledge and information, I consider this suggestion totally impracticable. The only workable formula in this context is 'rights for peace'. Its greatest benefit would be that by accepting it the Arabs would immediately be able to find a starting point for a better future. At the moment, the Palestinian movement is caught in a blind alley, but by accepting the notion of ensuring peace on their being given their rights, the deadlock would instantly be broken and the Arabs would see before them a golden opportunity to begin their journey on the highway of progress.

On the issue of Palestine, all the Muslim leaders, Arabs and non-Arabs alike, have only one thing to say, and that is that Israel should return the land occupied during the war and only then will the Palestinians stop all violent activities. Acceptance of this proposal is supposed to lead to 'peace with justice'.

As we know, despite a huge amount of effort, it has never been possible to put this proposal into effect. The sole reason for the failure of this formula is that it is unrealistic. No unrealistic formula can ever meet with success in this world of realities. This world being based on the eternal laws of nature, only that formula can meet with success which is reinforced by these laws.

The truth is that according to the laws of nature, justice is not a part of peace; therefore, bracketing justice with peace may have meaning in terms of human aspirations, but it is a fallacy from the point of view of reality. Once peace is established, justice is not an automatic sequel. It only opens opportunities. The task of achieving justice begins when we grasp these opportunities to establish it. The truth is that whenever one receives justice, it is the result of one's own hard work—whether acting as individuals or as groups. Prophet Muhammad provides a very clear historical example of this in his method of negotiating the Hudaybiyya peace treaty (as we saw in chapter 20).

By the grace of God I have travelled to Palestine three times, in August 1995, in October 1997 and then again in October 2008. These visits gave me the opportunity to observe Palestine at first hand. Moreover, I have met a number of Palestinian Muslims in and outside Delhi, and have also familiarized myself with their situation by reading a number of authoritative books on Palestine.

In terms of my own experience, I can clearly say that the Palestinians are a vibrant people, possessed of great potential, both physical and intellectual. This is but natural, for they have been brought up in a geographical region which the Quran (17:1) describes as having been 'blessed' by the Almighty.

The Palestinians, endowed with exceptional natural qualities, are capable of undertaking great tasks, but it is very tragic that it has not been possible for them to realize their own potential. The principal reason for this tragedy is that their leaders have launched them on the path of violence and hatred. They have wrongly come to regard the land they are struggling for as of the greatest importance and are sacrificing their lives to acquire it. They are unaware of the fact that the life of a Palestinian is a thousand times more precious than the land which they have been making futile efforts to acquire for so long. Had Palestinians been aware of the possibilities of the modern age, they would certainly have availed of the opportunities it offered, and not only at the level of Palestine, but also at an international level. They would thus have made great progress.

Peaceful action, in accordance with the laws of nature, increases human creativity and is therefore at all times and in every way superior to violent action. Those who employ peaceful means for achieving their goals steadily evolve into creative groups. On the contrary, those who opt for the way of hatred and violence perpetually suffer from an erosion of their creativity, and it is almost impossible to compensate for the various kinds of losses resulting from their violence. While success crowns the actions of the creative groups in this world, uncreative groups are destined for every kind of failure. This is an eternal law of nature. There is no exception to it.

In conclusion, I would like to say that Islam is a peaceful religion, in the full sense of the term. We would not be wrong in saying that Islam is the first religious system in human history which offers a complete ideology of peace. By adopting it, Prophet Muhammad successfully brought about a peaceful revolution in the real sense. The ideology of Islam banishes the notion that there can be anything acceptable about terrorism. Islam is a completely peaceful religion and the Islamic method is a peaceful method. By following the ideology of peace, each individual's mind can be re-engineered away from the culture of violence and closer to the culture of peace.

The essence of Islamic teaching on the subject of peace is underscored by an incident that took place when Prophet Muhammad returned from the Tabuk campaign in 9 AH. When, along with his 30,000 companions, he reached Madinah, he said to one of them, 'We have come back from a smaller jihad to a greater jihad.'[3]

What did the Prophet mean by 'a smaller jihad' and 'a greater jihad'?

'A smaller jihad' connotes a temporary jihad and 'a greater jihad' connotes a permanent jihad. A permanent jihad is one which is a part of the daily life of a believer. In this present world, where man is undergoing a divine test, a believer has to lead a principled life, eschewing all kinds of temptations and provocations, and adhering with unflagging zeal to Islamic principles. That is why it is called a greater jihad.

So far as the smaller jihad is concerned, it is, in fact, another name for defensive war. It takes place infrequently and only as the occasion warrants it. It is not a permanent feature of Islamic life.

Prophet Muhammad was born in AD 570. He received his prophethood on 12 February 610 in Makkah. He died on 8 June 632 in Madinah. Thus his prophetic period, according to the Christian calendar, lasted twenty-two years and three months. In this entire period, only four short battles took place: the Battle of Badr (2 AH); the Battle of Uhud (3 AH); the Battle of Khaybar (7 AH); and the Battle of Hunayn (8 AH). On all these four occasions, the battles, or rather skirmishes, lasted for only half a day. That is, two days in total. If you count the days of his prophetic period, the total comes to about 8130 days. So during this long period, the Prophet and his companions were engaged in peaceful struggle for 8128 days and they fought defensive battles for only two days. It would thus be appropriate to say that, in Islam, peace is the rule and war the rare exception.

29

The Difference between Islam and Muslims

One who wants to understand Islam is always faced with a problem. On the one hand, he finds the Quran, the scriptures of Islam, and on the other, he finds the Muslims who claim to be the followers of Islam. He forms opinions on Islam after studying Muslim behaviour. This is a common mistake committed by seekers of the truth. Therefore, the first guiding principle for the student of Islam is to differentiate between Islam and Muslims. Muslims must be judged in the light of Islamic teachings, and not vice versa.

The truth is that Islam is a religious ideology, whereas the position of Muslims is determined by the sentiments and conduct of a community.

This is a basic principle to be observed if the study of Islam is to be scientific. Keeping this in view, one can form a correct opinion of Islam. If this principle is neglected, any opinion one forms will not be factual.

The Politics of Reaction

The twentieth century saw the rise of movements whose objective was to establish the political and legal systems of

Islam, for example, the movements led by Sayyid Qutb in the Arab world, Sayyid Abul Ala Maududi on the Indian subcontinent, Abdul Qahhar Muzakkir in Indonesia, Saeed Naurasi in Turkey and Hasan Turabi in Sudan. These leaders launched their campaigns for the political revival of Islam through their speeches and writings.

All the political movements of this kind were reactionary in essence. They were produced in reaction to colonial rule. They were, in fact, national and political movements, but to make them popular among the masses, the leaders made their case by using Islamic terminology.

At the time of the rise of the colonial powers, the major part of the world was ruled by the Muslims—the Mughal empire on the subcontinent, the Ottoman empire in Turkey, the Safavid empire in Iran as well as large areas in Asia and Africa were under Muslim rule. When the colonial powers entered the Muslim world, the Muslim empires of those times wanted to check this onslaught, but the colonial powers, strong both militarily and economically, were able to vanquish their adversaries in every field. The Muslim leaders found this state of affairs unbearable and therefore took up arms against them.

This struggle started off peacefully; for instance, Sayyed Abul Ala Maududi wrote extensively emphasizing that political power was a prerequisite for the survival of Islam and his writing was disseminated on a large scale.

The establishment of the state of Israel in 1948 in Palestine was intolerable to the Muslims. To the writer, however, this was not wrong in principle, and was not a wrong decision, for, according to the Balfour Declaration, under the limited quota system, the Jews were allowed to return to one part of Palestine. These Jews were, in fact, the same who were in the Diaspora. And according to the Quran (5:21), the return of the Jews of the Diaspora was right in principle. But the Muslims, already enraged at the Western nations because of the colonial yoke they had imposed, now became bent on waging a war against them.

These movements, aimed at political jihad, initially employed peaceful methods, but when peaceful methods were not successful, they launched armed movements in the name of jihad. But again, when these leaders saw that they were not achieving success even through armed jihad, they resorted to suicide bombing. Suicide bombing is undoubtedly unlawful in Islam, but the Muslim leaders gave it a good name—*istishhaad* (seeking martyrdom)—and thus, for their part, legitimized it for themselves.

Now the position at the beginning of the twenty-first century is that, despite armed jihad and suicide bombing, the Muslims leaders have failed to achieve their objective. Moreover, this violent course of action has proved counterproductive, for the Muslims have not only failed to achieve anything by engaging in it, but have lost whatever they already had.

When we look at this situation in the light of purely Islamic teachings, we must say perforce that the reaction of the Muslim leaders, whether directed against the colonial system or against Israel, was based not on the teachings of Islam but on a deviation from them. The movements of

Muslim leaders turned in the wrong direction and went against the law of nature. That is why they have not been able to attain their goal.

Referring to a similar situation, a clearly worded verse in the Quran offers what is, in effect, a law of nature as a guiding principle:

'We bring these days to men by turns.' (3:140)

That is, political power is not a monopoly of a certain group. Political power will be given to different groups by turn. In other words, reacting against a change in political power is not a correct policy.

This teaching of the Quran does not advise cowardice or surrender. It is, in fact, based on a superior wisdom. It means that instead of negative reaction, the situation should be faced with positive planning.

Whenever there is a change in political power, it is not just a mere change, but it heralds the emergence of new opportunities. It is a manifestation of the law of nature established by God Himself. Whenever any nation has been in possession of political power for a long period of time, stagnation sets in among the people and their creativity declines. In such a situation, political change is required to raise the people out of the doldrums—to present them with fresh challenges and to bring about a new awakening. Every group, after enjoying political power for a long period of time, lapses into an uncreative state. This being so, a change in political power is necessary to turn it back into a creative group.

Had Muslim leaders understood this law of nature, they would have realized that the best solution for them lay in avoiding the course of reaction. They should have taken the change as a challenge and faced it peacefully, in a positive frame of mind, just as Japan successfully faced the challenge posed by America in the Second World War. But the Muslim leaders failed to understand this peaceful course of action. They fell prey to negative reaction. It is a fact that in this world, positive reaction yields positive result, whereas negative reaction yields negative result. This is an eternal law of nature and no group is an exception to this rule.

The Cartoon Issue

The way Muslims made an issue of a cartoon of the Prophet published in a local newspaper of Denmark, *Jyllands Posten*, and staged violent protests, was unrelated to Islam. The said cartoon was simply a journalistic joke, which is common in journalism. But the way Muslims reacted to it, displaying hatred and violence, was undoubtedly in violation of the teachings of the Prophet and an abuse of what the Prophet stood for.

A study of the life of the Prophet shows that such incidents repeatedly took place throughout his life. But he invariably ignored all such matters.[1]

One of the teachings of the Prophet of Islam is about distancing oneself from all such acts that distorted the image of Islam. The present age is one of freedom of expression. And displaying such violent reactions will certainly create the impression that Islam is against freedom of expression. In such a situation, creating a furore on such issues cannot be lawful on any pretext. No excuse can justify such violence. Even if Muslim sentiments are hurt, Muslims must opt for a policy of avoidance of confrontation. The plea of hurt sentiments cannot serve as an excuse for violence.

The Veil

In the Prophet's time, men and women were considered equal. The present form of veil or purdah did not exist, the veil as we know it having been developed in later times. The Prophet once observed, 'Women are half of men.'[2] That is to say, men and women are two equal halves of a single unit.

On the question of the status of the sexes vis-à-vis each other, Islam is basically against mixed society, holding that it is unnatural for men and women to have a common workplace. Similarly, nudity also goes against the teachings of Islam. It is a principle of Islam that men and women should lead married lives and that when a woman goes out she should be decently dressed. Her body should be covered up, except for her hands, feet and face. Women are allowed to go to the mosque to say their prayers but, for the sake of discipline, their rows are arranged separately from men's. The teachings of Islam about the status and role of men and women can be summed up in these words: 'Equal in respect but different in role.'

The Five Schools of Jurisprudence

At present, Muslims subscribe to five major schools of jurisprudence: Maliki, Hambali, Shafei, Hanafi and Jafri. All these schools of law relate to one and the same religion, yet that one religion has, in reality, been divided into five separate religions. How has this happened? What is the reason for so many differences that have led to factions and divisions and confrontations of an extreme nature? A book written by the famous eleventh-century Maliki scholar Muhammad ibn Abdul Bar titled *Jami'-al-Bayan al 'Ilm wa Fazlihi* throws light on this issue. The crux of the matter, which is explained in this and other books on the subject, will be summed up here.

Like other religious systems, there are two parts to the religious teachings of Islam—basic and non-basic. It has to be understood at the outset that, in the first phase of Islam (the period of the Prophet, of the companions of the Prophet, of the disciples of the companions of the Prophet), both forms of teachings—basic and non-basic—existed. And in this period, these two parts did not cause any schism. It was only during the Abbasid period that these differences led to a division. As we know, Islamic sciences were developed during the Abbasid period and it was in this period that the traditions of the Prophet were extensively collected. Inter alia, these traditions explain how the Prophet used to pray. They tell of how there were certain observances of the ritual of prayer which the companions of the Prophet followed in an identical manner; for instance, all the companions said two units for *fajr* (dawn prayer), four units for *zuhr* (noon prayer), four units for *'asr* (afternoon prayer), three units for *maghrib* (sunset prayer) and four units for *'isha* (evening prayer); whereas in other observances, there were differences. For instance, some folded their hands on the chest while beginning the prayer, some did so below the chest; some said 'Amen' quietly after the recitation of the first chapter 'al-Fatiha', while others said it loudly; and while saying 'Allahu Akbar', some raised their hands, and others did not.

All these differences came to light when the traditions were collected. Now the question arose as to how to explain them. Removing all the differences was not possible, for the source of all these differences were the Prophet's companions who had directly observed the Prophet's way of worship. The Prophet had said to his companions, 'Pray as you see me pray.' In such a situation, every method was authentic in its nature. Evidently, it proved difficult to determine what should be the basis for adopting one way and not another, and the Muslim jurists remained divided. The opinion of one was, 'Truth cannot be many' (*al haqqu la yatáaddad*). So, for practical purposes, the principle of preference was adhered to. That is, one opinion was preferred over another.

But this principle notwithstanding, the problem could not be solved. For, the principle of preference is always based on ijtihaad, and where ijtihaad has to be resorted to, there will always be a difference of opinion. Therefore, several opinions were formed, with each of their proponents insisting on their veracity and the correctness of their stand.

In this way, they were divided into groups. This is the reason behind the existence of the various schools of fiqh.

Discussing this principle of preference, Muhammad bin Idris Ash-Shafi had aptly commented in the ninth century that his opinion was right, with the possibility of that being wrong, and the opinion of others was wrong, with the possibility of that being right. Judging by these words of Imam Shafi, we see how illogical the viewpoint of the Muslim jurists was. Even after one opinion was given preference, there was still the possibility of its being wrong, and even after one opinion was abandoned, there was still the possibility of its being right, so that expressing any preference at all became totally meaningless. Given this state of affairs, it would become impossible for anyone to be able to worship with full conviction. And it is beyond doubt that, in such matters as worship, the element of conviction is essential.

We can understand the viewpoint of the traditionists from the answer given by Imam Ahmad ibn Hambal (d. 855) to Muhammad bin Abdur Rahman Sairafi when the latter asked, 'If on some matter we find the companions holding different opinions, should we try to analyse them to know the truth of the matter and only then follow it?' Imam Ahmad replied, 'No.' When asked once again what should be done in such a case, he replied, 'You may opt for any saying of any companion and follow that accordingly.'[3]

The essence of the traditionists' standpoint is that they attributed the difference in traditions to diversity. That is, either of the opinions could be right. This concept was directly derived from this tradition of the Prophet of Islam:

'My companions are like stars, whoever you follow, you will be guided.'[4]

The wisdom of this viewpoint was that in everything there were some elements which were basic and some which were non-basic. It is a general principle that oneness is desirable only in basic matters and not in non-basic ones. In non-basic matters, there is always diversity; in the absence of diversity in non-basic issues, rigidity will take over. And rigidity is never desirable, whatever the issue.

Furthermore, worship of God is another name for a living action. It is not an enactment of some spiritless deed. When worship is performed in right earnest, there can be uniformity only insofar as the basic elements are concerned but, as regards non-basic elements, diversity will be automatically produced. A living act of worship cannot be confined to one method. Trying to introduce uniformity into something non-basic is to turn worship into a set of empty rituals. Such worship can be likened to the actions of a mechanical robot rather than to the actions of a living human being. Worship is an act performed with elevated spiritual feelings, and such an act can never follow the total uniformity of a spiritless ritual.

When we study the traditions of the companions of the Prophet on the subject of worship, we find that their worship was uniform as regards the basics, but there was diversity as regards the non-basic elements. Here is an example that explains the nature of the worship performed by the companions. According to a tradition narrated by a companion of the Prophet, Rifaah ibn Rafi al-Ansari

(d. 661), one day when the Prophet was leading the sunset (maghrib) prayer, he said the words *Sami' Allahu liman hamidah* while kneeling, and a person who was saying the prayer behind the Prophet added these words on his own: *Rabbana wa lakal hamd, hamdan kathiran tayyiban mubarakan fih* (O my Lord, Praise be to You, abundance of Praise, Holy, Blessed).

When the prayer was concluded, the Prophet satisfied himself as to who had said those words, and said: 'I saw 30 angels wanting to be the first to record those words.'[5]

There are many such incidents recorded in the books of the Hadith relating to the Prophet and his companions. These incidents show that there is no set formula for the non-basic elements of the prayer. Prayer is a living act and no living act can follow a set pattern. A living act is replete with feeling and as such can never conform to a rigid orthodoxy.

So far as the basic structure of prayer is concerned, there will always be uniformity, but the non-basic parts of prayer inevitably come under the sway of inner feelings. In non-basic matters, feeling will be expressed in a variety of ways. The truth is that making prayer conform to a uniform structure in all its aspects is against the spirit of worship and also runs counter to the example of the Prophet and his companions.

History tells us that in the times of the *muhaddithin* (traditionists) all these different schools of fiqh did not exist. These schools of law were formed subsequently in the period of the jurists. In the initial stage, the existence of different legal schools seemed to present no great difficulties, but, gradually, after some centuries had elapsed, their differences assumed an extreme form, a form for which, according to the Quran and the Hadith, there is no room in Islam.

Implementation of the Shariah Law

In present times, movements to impose shariah law have been launched in Muslim countries such as Afghanistan, Iran, Sudan and Pakistan. In all these countries, we find almost the same state of affairs. Muslims are divided into two groups—the ruler and the ruled. These two groups have gone on a collision course, resulting in great harm. It has ultimately proved impossible to impose the shariah law, and these movements have only brought hatred, violence and coercion in their wake.

Why did these movements to impose Islamic law prove to be counterproductive? The reason is that everywhere the watchword was the enforcement of shariah law, where the example of introducing change by a gradual process as set by the Prophet of Islam was not followed.

The Prophet of Islam lived as a prophet in this world for a period of twenty-three years. One part of his mission was to enforce Islamic law in Arabia, and he succeeded in doing so. But in that period, we do not find Muslims in Arabia dividing themselves into groups and fighting in the name of the enforcement of the shariah, like the Muslims of today.

A tradition of the Prophet narrated by Aisha, the Prophet's wife, sheds light on the nature of this problem. She says:

'First of all, those verses were revealed in the Quran which deal with God and the Hereafter. It was only when people had come within the fold of Islam, and minds had been prepared, that the commands concerning what was lawful and unlawful were revealed. If the commands regarding the prohibition of wine and adultery had been revealed first, people would certainly have said, "We will never stop drinking and we will never stop committing adultery."'[6]

According to a tradition, everyone is born a child of nature. But then, under the influence of the environment, he or she gradually turns away from the natural state. This is known as perversion. The act of forming a good society begins with the rectifying of this perversion—that is, bringing the state of perversion to an end and causing people to revert to their original state.[7] This process of rectification may be categorized as de-conditioning.

According to the tradition narrated by Aisha, the way of Prophet Muhammad was first to de-condition people and then bring them back to their original state. The successful completion of this process engenders in members of society the capacity to readily accept the commandments concerned. And it is only then that the task of enforcing shariah law can be properly performed. According to the method of the Prophet of Islam, the enforcement of shariah law begins in any society with intellectual purification, rather than with the practical enforcement of the law.

Today, there are fifty-seven Muslim countries, in every one of which Muslim leaders have launched a movement for the enforcement of the shariah. But even after a long struggle, these movements have failed to achieve their goal. All they have succeeded in doing is create traditions of violence and coercion.

In this regard, Muslim countries can be divided into two groups. One group consists of those where violent confrontation is going on between the ruler and the ruled, and the other consists of those where an oppressive, coercive system has been put in place. The latter are the countries where the rulers have suppressed these movements and established their rule by the use of force. Obviously, both these situations are undesirable from the Islamic viewpoint.

Had the Muslims in question followed the method of the Prophet, they would have learnt that the right way of working was for their leaders to begin their work from the non-political field. By imparting peaceful training, these leaders could have reformed the mind and character of the people. While doing this, they could have opted for the way of status-quoism regarding the political system of the country. They could have subordinated matters of politics and government to the democratic process. They could have given the people the opportunity to elect their representatives by the peaceful, democratic procedure of voting, thus giving them their share in governance.

Had the Muslim leaders opted for this path of wisdom, certainly the conditions would gradually have changed. In these countries, first of all, a revolution in terms of thinking and character would have been brought about and then gradually politics and government too would have been revolutionized. But because of their blindness to prophetic wisdom, the leaders have not only failed to achieve their objective, but they have also incurred great losses within Muslim society.

There are a number of traditions in the books of the Hadith which expressly command Muslims not to, under any circumstances, opt for a collision course with their rulers, however much perversion has set in in them. If they think that something needs to be done to rectify matters, they should advise the leaders of this in private. Such movements should never be aimed at confrontation with the rulers.

This policy of non-confrontation does not mean surrender. It means to remain strictly peaceful and continue to strive to educate people in non-political spheres. This allows time for decisions to be taken about what action is necessary, if any, when it becomes evident that political perversion has taken place. Efforts to resolve the problem without resorting to confrontation should be continued till conditions improve to the extent that the desired change can be effected peacefully.

The policy of Islam in all matters is based on result-oriented action, and that too action that yields positive results. Only if the result of an action is going to be positive should one go ahead; if the result is likely to be counterproductive, one had better opt for the way of peaceful reform, keeping oneself totally away from politics. With the adoption of this method, peace will necessarily prevail, whereas going against this method will inevitably result in war and violence.

The Issue of Abuse of the Prophet

Muslims believe in general that, judging by the Islamic shariah, the punishment of one who abuses the Prophet should be death. If you ask them to substantiate this claim, they will immediately refer to fiqh. They will say that it is an accepted ordinance in Islamic fiqh that anyone held to have been abusing the Prophet should be executed.

This kind of reference in itself is baseless: killing a person comes under capital punishment and a law of this nature has to be derived directly from the Quran and the Hadith, the source books in Islam, rather than from some discipline developed later on the basis of interpretation. It is an established fact that in Islam only the Quran and the Hadith have the position of authentic sources. No third source is legally tenable. So far as fiqh is concerned, it is totally based on qayas (inference). And inferences made by the scholars can never be an accepted source in any law.

The issue of shatm-ar-rasul (abuse of the Prophet) has been discussed in the books of law and a number of books have been written exclusively on this subject. Some of these are Al-Sarimul-Maslul 'ala Shatimir-Rasul by Taqiuddin Ahmad ibn Taimiyya (d. 1328); Al-Saiful-maslul 'ala man Sabbar-Rasul by Taqiuddin Abul-Hasan Ali bin Abdul-Kafi Al-Subuki (d. 1355); and Tambihul-wulat wal-Hukkam 'ala Ahkami Shatimi Khairil-Anaam by S. Muhammad Amin bin Umar al-Shami (d. 1836).

Regarding the punishment for those who abuse the Prophet, Muslims are very sensitive. But all the books written on this subject carry no valid reference from the Quran and the Hadith.

The first question to be asked in this regard is: which verse of the Quran gives the injunction to kill the abuser of the Prophet? In all the chapters of the Quran with their hundreds of verses, there is not a single verse which gives the command to kill an abuser of the Prophet.

Those who support the slaying of the Prophet's abuser cite certain verses of the Quran, but these are totally irrelevant to the issue concerned. For instance, ibn Taimiyya quotes in his book *Al-Sarimul-Maslul 'ala Shatimir-Rasul* certain verses, one of which is:

'Those who annoy God's messenger will have a painful punishment.' (9:61)

The 'painful punishment' mentioned in this verse of the Quran clearly refers to the punishment in the life after death, rather than punishment in this world. It is extremely unscientific to fail to differentiate between punishment in this world and in the next world. Punishment in this world is the result of a sentence pronounced in a human court, whereas punishment in the next life will result directly from the divine verdict. These punishments differ entirely from one another in nature. The argument that a Quranic verse equates retribution in the afterlife with punishment in this world is totally without logic.

The second source of the Islamic shariah is the sayings and deeds of the Prophet. But here, those who advocate the killing of any abuser of the Prophet will not find one single

Hadith to support their argument. They might establish their stand if they could quote a tradition of the Prophet which clearly says, 'Anyone who abuses your Prophet should be killed.' But it can be said with certainty that in the whole body of Hadith literature, no such authentic tradition has been recorded by anyone.

Imam Muhamamd bin Ahmad Az Zahbi (d. 1348) wrote, 'A Hadith which is not known to ibn Taimiyya is not an authentic Hadith.' But even ibn Taimiyya, renowned as a great religious scholar, failed to present an authentic Hadith to this effect.

In his book ibn Taimiyya quotes a tradition, the authenticity of which he himself was not quite certain about. Its wording is as follows, 'Anyone who abuses any of the prophets should be killed.' Ibn Taimiyya himself wrote of this Hadith that it was possibly fabricated, and that only if its authenticity were proved could it serve as an argument that the abusers of the prophets should be killed.

Now even 700 years after the publication of ibn Taimiyya's book, no scholar has yet written about the source and authenticity of this tradition. In such a case, it can be concluded with certainty that it is a fabricated Hadith. And a fabricated Hadith does not prove anything.

The above argument thus makes it clear that the Quran and the Hadith have not given a command to kill an abuser of the Prophet.

According to a tradition, a poet belonging to a polytheistic tribe once came to Prophet Muhammad in Madinah to express his thoughts on polytheism. This he did in the form of couplets. (Before the age of the press, people generally gave expression to their thoughts in poetry. That is to say, poetry enjoyed the position of the media in those times.) In order to counter the poet, the Prophet sent for Hassan ibn Thabit, also a poet. When Hassan came to the Prophet, he said to him, 'Hassan, rise and answer this man.' Then Hassan stood up and answered him in the form of couplets.

We find many such incidents in the life of the Prophet. This shows that if anyone says anything against Islam or the Prophet, the counter-action will be at an equal level, that is, word for word and writing for writing. This shows that retaliating against the pen with the sword is not the way of Islam. Any such incident relating to the use of the pen against Islam should be for Muslims an intellectual challenge—it is in no way a military challenge. On such occasions, the opposite party has to be satisfied with arguments and reasoning in peaceful ways; satisfying the other party at an intellectual level is the rule. In such situations, resorting to violence can never be justified.

The Preservation of Culture

The destruction of the Buddha statues in Bamiyan in 2001 by the Taliban has fostered a widespread belief that Islam does not set store by cultural heritage. The modern world places utmost importance on historical monuments, regardless of the countries to which they belong. The Islamic tradition, no less than other traditions and disciplines, attaches great importance to cultural heritage, or historical monuments. The preservation of cultural heritage, in fact, is related to the general matters of humanity, where there is no difference between the secular and the Islamic point of view. According to Islam, historical monuments are indeed worthy of being preserved, as they are indispensable records of the past. If these records were not to be maintained, future generations would lose authentic sources of knowledge. It would be an irremediable loss.

Islam is a religion of nature. Everything which is in accordance with nature—as also reason—is regarded as important in Islam. One important and accepted principle of the Islamic shariah holds that 'all things, in essence, are lawful, when not forbidden'. Looked at in the light of this shariah principle, the preserving of a cultural heritage is certainly lawful in Islam; nowhere in the Quran or Sunnah are we commanded not to preserve our cultural heritage. Since we are not forbidden to do so, such preservation becomes lawful per se. No other proof is required on this count.

Moreover, when we study the Quran, we find references regarding the importance of cultural inheritance. One such verse in the Quran says:

'Bring me a scripture revealed before this, or any other remnant of knowledge you may have, if you are telling the truth!' (46:4)

In my opinion, what is meant by 'remnant of knowledge' is what, in today's jargon, we would call an archaeological or historical record. Such records serve as vital sources from which to learn about past events; therefore it becomes essential to preserve them, both from the academic and the Islamic point of view.

One significant example of the importance of preserving a cultural or historical record is found in the Quran in relation to the Pharaoh, the Egyptian king and Moses' contemporary, who died by drowning. The Quran makes this statement about him:

> 'So We shall save your body this day, so that you may serve as a sign for those who come after you.'
> (10:92)

The body of this Pharaoh was embalmed according to Egyptian custom and entombed in a pyramid. The embalmed body, a part of the Egyptian culture, remained preserved for posterity by the will of God Himself. At the end of the nineteenth century, when the mummy was removed from its tomb and the modern method of carbon dating was applied on it to determine its age, it was proved that the mummy was the earthly remains of the same Pharaoh who had been drowned during the time of Prophet Moses. The preserved mummy of this Pharaoh, still in existence at a museum in Cairo, bears witness to the veracity of the above Quranic verse. Despite the Pharaoh being an idolatrous king, God willed that his body be preserved. This clearly shows us that Islam not only allows common things pertaining to cultural history to be preserved but also the body of an idolatrous king! We can therefore safely infer that the preservation of the Buddha statues in Afghanistan, which dated back 2000 years, was as valued in Islam as it was in other traditions and disciplines.

In the context of the history of the Israelites, the Quran tells us that they possessed a sacred relic (the Ark of the Covenant), a part of their heritage which they preserved for generations as a source of peace and security. This relic, or cultural legacy, was first preserved by the generations of Moses and Aaron. We learn from the Quran (2:248) that such great importance was attached to this inherited Ark that, on one occasion, it was borne aloft by the angels from one place to another!

This incident is a direct illustration of the preservation of cultural heritage. This underscores the importance of cultural heritage as well as the fact that such preservation for the benefit of coming generations does not run counter to the spirit of the divine shariah.

An important attribute of a believer, as described in the Quran, is that of a traveller (9:112), that is, one who travels the land from one place to another to take lessons from historical places. As the Quran in another verse says:

'How many townships have We destroyed where the people had become arrogant on account of their affluence? Since then their dwelling-places have scarcely been inhabited—We became their inheritors'. (28:58)

It also says:

'Say, "Travel about the land and see what was the end of the deniers."' (6:11)

According to these verses, it is desirable in Islam to preserve the cultural heritage of the past in order that the coming generations may derive lessons from them. In the absence of such historical relics, the very purpose of travelling would be rendered meaningless.

Every group or community has its own particular culture. And it possesses the absolute right to safeguard it. In matters relating to culture, the question of whether it is against or in favour of Islam should not arise. Indeed, any community that wants to protect its culture should be given the right to do so: just as this tenet has been endorsed by secularism, so has it been accepted by Islam.

There is an event in Islamic history which very aptly illustrates this point. Jerusalem was conquered during the caliphate of Umar, the second caliph of Islam. Caliph Umar went to Jerusalem from Makkah, and signed an agreement with the Christians. This agreement contained, among other things, the guarantee that all the relics in the Christian churches—for instance, the statues of Mary and Jesus, and the Holy Cross, believed to be the one on which Christ was nailed—would be left intact. All these objects were part of the Christian culture, and it was specified in the agreement that the Christian community had the right to preserve and maintain them.[8]

This act on the part of the second caliph of Islam shows that it is the right of every community to safeguard its culture, whether under Muslim rule or not. No government is vested with the right to interfere in the cultural affairs of a community. The issue of preservation of culture must remain independent of government intervention. One important point to be borne in mind is that, as far as international matters are concerned, the Islamic norm would be the same as that agreed upon by all nations. This principle of Islam is established from the life of the Prophet.

According to the Quran and the life of the Prophet, if any principle has been accepted at the international level, it has to be followed, such as in the case of the preservation of cultural heritage. In the modern world, great stress indeed is laid upon the preservation of cultural legacies or historical monuments, and Islam has no quarrel with this. It will certainly never follow a divergent course on matters of common consent.

Let us take a relevant example from the life of the Prophet. The Prophet of Islam was born in Makkah where there were no date palms. When he migrated to Madinah, he found date orchards in abundance. One day, as the Prophet was passing by an orchard, he saw some men high up in the palm trees, pollinating them with their hands. The Prophet said that he did not think there was any particular advantage in doing this and advised them to give up this practice. That year, the yield of dates was very low. When the Prophet asked why this was so, he was told that since he had discouraged the owners of the trees from pollinating them, the yield of dates had fallen. At this, the Prophet said:

'Continue to do what you have been doing, for you know your worldly matters better.'9

This particular advice given by the Prophet points to a very important principle. It concerns the necessity to differentiate between matters of creed and practicalities. According to Islam, practical matters, which are of a purely worldly nature, are not to be subordinated to religion. They have to be instead subjected to academic research and judged by experience. Those which satisfy the academic criteria will gain general acceptance as standard concepts and practices. This includes the various disciplines ranging from agriculture to horticulture, as well as all the departments of engineering and history. Thus, the preservation of historical legacies falls within the province of academic research rather than that of religion.

All this is to say that if a non-Muslim cultural heritage, considered at variance with Islamic interests, exists in some Muslim country the people of that country are not authorized to destroy it, simply by virtue of their being in political control. They should rather hand over the symbols to whichever countries that wish to preserve them. The demolition of the Buddhist statues at Bamiyan in Afghanistan was totally against Islam. It was an act of extremism, and according to both the Quran and the Hadith, extremism has neither basis nor sanction in Islam.

To sum up, the principles of Islam and their practical applications both demonstrate that, in matters regarding the preservation of cultural or historical heritage, the stance adopted by Islam is the same as that of other traditions and disciplines.

Conclusion

Many historians have acknowledged that the Prophet of Islam achieved extraordinary success in his life. For instance, Michael Hart states in his book, *The 100*,[1] that Prophet Muhammad was supremely successful on both the religious and the secular levels, and places him right at the top of his list of the one hundred most illustrious names in the entire range of human history. But this author does not tell us how the Prophet of Islam managed to achieve this extraordinary success. The secret lay in his being perhaps the first person in history who adopted the principle of 'peace for the sake of peace'. He went out of his way to follow this policy of peace throughout his life, contrary to the misconception that a significant part of his life was spent in waging wars. The Prophet also made the important point that peace in itself does not necessarily lead us to our goals. It rather opens the door to opportunities, by availing of which we can achieve our desired goals.

The Prophet of Islam was the Prophet of Peace, in the full sense of the expression. All his teachings, directly or indirectly, are based on peace. The few 'battles' that took place throughout his life were purely defensive in nature. These were of such short duration that they could more appropriately be called skirmishes. The Second World War lasted six years, whereas the total duration of the Prophet's 'battles' was less than six days.

Political power was not the goal of the Prophet of Islam. The actual goal of his prophetic mission was to help people to lead their lives in accordance with the straight path laid down by God, so that they might have an eternal share in God's mercy.

When this objective of the Prophet of Islam's mission is borne in mind, it becomes abundantly clear that the Prophet of Islam was indeed the Prophet of Peace. In the religion brought by him, peace was the rule and war was the rare exception, a measure to be resorted to as an unavoidable option in the case of armed aggression by an attacker.

The Prophet Muhammad demonstrated his profound wisdom in his method of negotiating the Hudaybiyya peace treaty. By unilaterally accepting the conditions of his opponents, he concluded a historic ten-year no-war pact, without apparently receiving justice or his rights. But, by means of this peace treaty, the Prophet and his companions were enabled to consolidate themselves so thoroughly that they had no need to wage war to attain justice.

The study of the Prophet's life shows that he never initiated a military move himself. When his opponents wanted to embroil him in war, he would on all occasions resort to some strategy of avoidance to avert war. He fought only when there was no other way left to him. According to the sunnah of the Prophet, there is no aggressive or offensive war in Islam. Islam allows only a defensive war and that, too, only when there is no other option.

But today, a section of Muslims have waged wars at different places. When they are asked, 'Don't you want peace?' they reply, 'We want peace, but we want peace with justice.' They add that if others will give them peace, they will give them justice in return. This goes wholly against the teachings of the Prophet of Islam. The Prophet's enemies had treated him with great injustice. But the Prophet never waged war against the injustices done to him and his companions. What he did, first of all, was to establish peace through unilateral adjustment. He later availed of the opportunities this offered to achieve his desired goals. It was this wise principle which the Prophet honoured throughout his entire life.

Our leaders of the present day have not thought fit to follow this principle. They have never tried to establish peace, being more intent on continuing to wage war on their supposed enemies in the name of putting an end to injustice. These wars, which are totally against the teachings of Islam, have proved futile, yielding no positive result whatsoever.

The truth is that the above-mentioned principle of the Prophet is not only a religious principle: it is also a law of nature. And it is a fact that in this world only those achieve success who follow the law of nature, while those who deviate from it are doomed to failure.

A tradition narrated by Ayesha, the Prophet's wife, provides a guiding principle. She said: 'Whenever the Prophet had to choose between two courses, he would always opt for the easier one.'[2] This means that whenever the Prophet had two options before him in any matter, he would always abandon the harder option in favour of the easier one.

This tradition (sunnah) of the Prophet Muhammad is relevant not only to everyday affairs but also to such serious matters as, by their very nature, entail more difficult options.

The truth is that in life we have to face the problem of choosing between two courses: between the confrontational and the non-confrontational, between the peaceful and the violent. The study of the Prophet's life tells us that the Prophet, in all matters, abandoned the violent or confrontational course in favour of the peaceful or non-confrontational course. The whole life of the Prophet provides a successful, practical example of this principle.

The Prophet of Islam brought an unprecedented revolution to the world, one that was initiated by a profound feeling of spiritual discovery, and accomplished by a unique display of positive virtues. Should anyone wish to achieve the same revolution from the negativity that comes from a sense of loss, he should have to find another God—for it is not God's will that this should happen. He should also have to find another prophet—for that was not the way of the Prophet.

The exemplary life the Prophet lived can serve as an unfailing guide to right thinking and right living in the modern age. Through his example, man can understand how to live in accordance with the creation plan of God. This is the greatest boon of the Prophet to the modern man. His teachings give man the opportunity to live his life in a far better way, and on a far higher plane.

Acknowledgements

The idea for this book arose out of a conversation I had a few years ago with the *Arab News* editor, Siraj Wahab; and Harun Shaikh, editor, *Spiritual Message*, Mumbai. They were of the view that I ought to write a book to spell out the misconceptions about Islam and the teachings of Prophet Muhammad on jihad against the backdrop of violence and terrorism which have become such a great menace to the world today. I therefore embarked upon the task of presenting the true teachings of Prophet Muhammad on non-violence. At the same time, I developed an ideology of peace based on the Quran and the Prophet's life and teachings.

During the preparation of this book, my daughter, Farida Khanam, made eminently useful suggestions about the different areas covered, particularly the spiritual themes. Her vast knowledge and keen interest have been of inestimable help. Indeed, many of the ideas in the book grew out of conversations with her.

Apart from her, Naghma Siddiqi, whom I consider, my 'spiritual daughter', was extremely helpful, thanks to her exhaustive knowledge of the subject, her grasp of detail and her extraordinary dedication.

I am thankful to Maulana Zakwan Nadvi, for checking the text thoroughly and correcting references, especially from the Hadith literature and other Islamic sources. I am also thankful to K.K. Sahadevan for patiently typing out the manuscript and adding corrections with meticulous accuracy.

My editors, Anna Khanna and Paul Joseph Menezes, provided very useful suggestions and considerably improved the language, grammar and style of the text.

Rajat Malhotra and my son, Saniyasnain Khan, and my granddaughter, Sadia Khan, were likewise very helpful in their enthusiastic commitment to the project.

And lastly, I should like to express my appreciation of the professional treatment the manuscript has received from the editorial team, in particular, Ranjana Sen Gupta and Jaishree Ram Mohan, who were assigned to the task by my publishers, Penguin Books.

May God bless them all!

Notes

Introduction

1. *Sahih*, Al-Bukhari, Hadith no. 28.
2. *Musnad Ahmad*, Vol. 3, p. 440.
3. *Sahih*, Al-Bukhari, Hadith no. 831.

The Islamic Model

1. Ismail ibn Kathir, *Al-Bidayah wan Nihayah*, Vol. 3, p. 214.
2. *Sahih*, Al-Bukhari, *Book of Funerals*, Hadith no. 1312.
3. *Hijrah* literally means 'the migration'. The Prophet emigrated from Makkah to Madinah in September 622. This year was later designated by Caliph Umar as the first year of the Islamic calendar, called Hijri calendar (AH).

A Prophet of Peace

1. Muslim ibn al-Hajjaj, *Book of Virtue*, Ch. 23, Hadith no. 2593.
2. Leo Tolstoy, *The Kingdom of God Is within You*, Ch. 10.
3. Ismail ibn Kathir, *Al-Bidayah wan Nihayah*, Vol. 3, p. 267.
4. *Musnad Ahmad*, Vol. 1, p. 307.
5. Muslim ibn al-Hajjaj, Hadith no. 104.
6. Ismail ibn Kathir, *Sirat ibn Kathir*, Vol. 1, p. 441.
7. *Musnad Ahmad*, Vol. 2, p. 297.

The Muslim Brotherhood

1. Richard Mitchell, *The Society of the Muslim Brothers*, London, Oxford University Press, 1969.

Political Extremism and Islam

1. *Musnad Ahmad*, Vol. 1, p. 215.

2. Abu Da'ud, *Sunan Abu Da'ud*, Book of Traditions, Vol. 1, p. 197; Hadith no. 4596.

3. *Sahih*, Al-Bukhari, Ch. 1, Hadith no. 1.

4. Albaihaqi, *Mishkat*, Hadith no. 276.

5. Amir Shakib Arsalan, *Our Decline: Its Causes and Remedies*, p. 47, Al Majlis-al-Ilmi, Delhi, 1993.

Analysing the Phenomenon of Terrorism

1. Philip K. Hitti, *History of the Arabs*, ch. 8, p. 111, London, Macmillan Press, 1937.

Countering the Terrorists' Ideology

1. Eugene Lyons, 'Milovan Djilas and the Book That Is Shaking the Communist World', *Reader's Digest*, October 1957.

2. Maulana Wahiduddin Khan, *Al-Risala*, p. 6, New Delhi, January 2005.

Does the Quran Support Terrorism?

1. Qurtubi, *Aljami Li Ahkaam Al-Quran* (1 / 263).

2. Fathul-Bari, Vol. 8, p. 32.

Negative Thinking Alien to Islam

1. Izzuddin ibn al-Asir, *Al-Kamil fi at Tarikh*, Vol. 12, p. 362.

2. *Diwan-e-Mirza*, Ch. 1.

Jihad or Terrorism

1. *Musnad Ahmad*, Vol. 6, p. 20.
2. *Sahih*, Al-Bukhari, Hadith no. 2957.
3. Ibn Hisham, *Life of the Prophet*, 4/98.
4. Ismail ibn Kathir, *Al-Bidayah wan Nihayah*, Vol. 5, p. 51.

Arguments against Suicide Bombing

1. Dr Yousuf Al-Qarzawi, *Al Mujtama*, 18 June 1996, pp. 34–35.
2. Ismail ibn Kathir, *Al-Bidayah wan Nihayah*, Vol. 6, p. 325.
3. Ibn Hajar al-Asqalani, *Fathul Bari*, Kitabul Maghazi, Vol. 7, p. 540.

Jihad against Muslim Rulers

1. *Sahih*, Al-Bukhari, *Book of the Holy War*, Hadith no. 2957.
2. *Musnad Ahmad*, Vol. 4, p. 416.
3. Al Tabrizi, *Mishkat al Masabih*, 2/1086.
4. *Musnad Ahmad*, Vol. 1, p. 384.
5. An Nawabi, *Commentary of Sahih Muslim*, Vol. 12, p. 229.

Who Are Kafirs?

1. *Musnad Ahmad*, Vol. 5, p. 181.

Democracy and Political Islam

1. Muslim ibn al-Hajjaj, *Sahih Muslim, Book of Faith*, Ch. no. 18, Hadith no. 46.
2. *Musnad Ahmad*, Vol. 1, p. 215.

Intellectual Development in Religion

1. *Muhaymin* is used here to describe the Quran as the determinant factor in deciding what is genuine and what is false.

2. Muslim ibn al-Hajjaj, *Book of Fate*, Ch. 6, Hadith no. 2658.

Islam and Modern Science

1. Ibn Hajar al-Asqalani, *Fathul Bari*, Vol. 3, p. 258.
2. Ibn Hajar al-Asqalani, *Fathul Bari*, Vol. 3, p. 261.
3. Julian Huxley, *Religion without Revelation*, London, 1957.

Who Is Dajjal?

1. *Sahih Muslim*, 'Kitabal Fitan'.
2. *Musnad Ahmad*, Vol. 2, p. 104.
3. *Al-Aimmatul Muzillun, Musnad Ahmad*, Vol. 1, p. 42.
4. *Sahih Muslim*, Hadith no. 115.
5. Kanzul-Ummal, Hadith no. 39709.
6. Ibn Rajab al-Hanbali al-Baghdadi, *Jamiul Uloom Wal Hikam*, p. 71.

An Abode of Peace

1. Abu Daud, Hadith no. 4291.

The Gifts from the West

1. For details see *The Bible, the Quran and Science*, Maurice Bucaille, American Trust Publication, 1978.
2. *Musnad Ahmad*, Vol. 6, p. 4.
3. Abu Daud, *Sunan Abu Daud, Book of Good Manners*, Vol. 4, p. 256.

The Problem of Palestine

1. Robert Briffault, *The Making of Humanity*, p. 190.
2. Philip K. Hitti, *History of the Arabs*, Macmillan Press, 1979.
3. *Kashful Khifa*, Vol. 2, p. 345.

The Difference between Islam and Muslims

1. See Maulana Wahiduddin Khan, 'Muslim Must Ignore Cartoons', 2 March 2006, *Pioneer*, New Delh.

2. *Musnad Ahmad*, Vol. 6, p. 256.

3. *Jami' Bayan al 'Ilm*, p. 83.

4. Kashful-Khifa, Vol. 1, p. 146.

5. *Sahih*, Al-Bukhari, Hadith No. 799.

6. *Sahih*, Al-Bukhari, *Kitab Fazail Al Quran*, Ch. 'Talif al Quran'.

7. *Sahih*, Al-Bukhari, Hadith No. 1385.

8. Abu Jafar Muhammad ibn Jarir al-Tabari, *Taarikh al Umam wa al Muluk*.

9. *Sahih Muslim*, Hadith no. 2363.

Conclusion

1. Hart, Michael H. *The 100: A Ranking of the Most Influential Persons in History.* New York: Carol Publishing Group / Citadel Press, 1978.

2. *Sahih Bukhari*, The Book of the Stories of the Prophets, Ch. 'The Description of the Prophet'. *Summarized Bukhari*, translated by Dr M. Muhsin Khan, p. 700, Hadith 1492.